How to Use Intervention in Your Professional Practice

How to Use Intervention in Your Professional Practice

A GUIDE FOR
HELPING-PROFESSIONALS
WHO WORK WITH
CHEMICAL DEPENDENTS
AND THEIR FAMILIES

JOHNSON INSTITUTE BOOKS

Professional Series
Minneapolis 1987

Published by Johnson Institute Books
510 First Avenue North
Minneapolis, Minnesota 55403.

Library of Congress Cataloging-in-Publication Data

How to use intervention in your professional practice.

(Professional series)
Includes index.
1. Substance abuse—Treatment. 2. Alcoholics—
Rehabilitation. 3. Narcotic addicts—Rehabilitation.
I. Johnson Institute (Minneapolis, Minn.) II. Series:
Professional series (Minneapolis, Minn.)
RC564.H68 1987   616.86′06   87-3406
ISBN 0-935908-41-2

PRINTED IN THE UNITED STATES OF AMERICA

10   9   8   7   6   5   4   3   2   1

ACKNOWLEDGMENTS

This book was written with the help of many past and present staff members of the Johnson Institute.

Special thanks are due to Karen Edens, Joseph Muldoon, René Sternau, and Mary Murck.

CONTENTS

PART 3: A MODEL FOR INTERVENTION PROGRAMMING

PART 4: SPECIAL ISSUES AND CONCERNS WITH INTERVENTION

PART 5: FURTHER RESOURCES FOR PROGRAMMING

INTRODUCTION

Here is a message to helping-professionals from Dr. Vernon E. Johnson, founder of the Johnson Institute and father of the intervention process.

In the early 1960s, intervention was a theory that seemed to fly in the face of long-established opinion and practice. When most people were saying that nothing could be done with alcoholics until they "hit bottom," some were getting alcoholics to accept help long before their lives had disintegrated. When popular opinion held that only chemically dependent people who were "self-motivated" would benefit from treatment, those practicing intervention were working effectively with the most deluded and resistant of addicts.

By the late 1970s, the process of intervention had gained widespread acceptance and was being practiced at virtually every economic and social level in the United States.

Today we face a new challenge. Never in living memory have alcohol and other drug abuse been so clearly a matter of national concern. Even our President and First Lady have assumed active and prominent leadership roles in the "War on Drugs." It would seem that those of us who have labored long in the field would feel relieved, even elated. Yet, quite to the contrary, many of us are uneasy, some of us are distressed. Not a few are downright alarmed as we see that once again our nation is trying to legislate chemical dependence away as though improvements in law enforcement can remove a deadly disease from our midst. We now see media spots that tell addicts who are ruining their lives that they should "just say no" to drugs—as though we believed they **could.**

We are saddened because such efforts ignore the lessons of history and serve to obscure the true nature of chemical dependence. When we look at the various attempts of legislators and media people to attack the problem, the old phrase comes to mind:

"When in danger, when in doubt,
Run in circles, scream and shout!"

Whatever happened to that virtual consensus of the 1930s when we all believed that Prohibition had caused more problems than it solved? Our nation has to realize, once again, that the disease itself renders the victims of chemical dependence less and less capable of a spontaneous recognition of the severity of their symptoms. Addicts who are ruining their lives cannot say "no" to drugs because they are incapable of comprehending what drugs are doing to them. **If they are to receive the insight they must have, that insight must come from those around them through conscious, planned, and caring acts of intervention.** We need to present reality in a receivable way to persons who are out of touch with it. We need to redirect our educational and counseling efforts to those who surround the suffering addicts— redirect them in ways that will mobilize these immobilized persons and help them become effective interveners in dealing with a disease that has become the number one scourge of our citizenry. Already, efforts at intervention have made significant inroads at all levels of our society, and as a result many thousands of persons are well and leading constructive lives.

For this we are grateful; but, all too clearly, there is much yet to be done.

These words by Dr. Vernon Johnson serve as a challenge to all of us helping-professionals who work with chemical dependents and their families. At no time in our history has professional education and training in intervention been more crucial. Ever since Dr. Johnson's first book on intervention, *I'll Quit Tomorrow,* was published in 1973, many successful interventions have been carried out—some with the assistance of helping-professionals, some without such help. Those helping-professionals who took the risks of intervening have learned much. But as they encountered special situations, new concerns and new questions have emerged.

This book is meant to serve as a guide for helping-professionals, a guide that provides them with the principles, guidelines, techniques, and strategies they need to guide families and others through interventions with alcohol/drug dependent persons. It also provides Johnson Institute's own intervention program model for professionals to use or adapt for use according to their particular cultural, social, logistical, and economic circumstances. The special section on issues and concerns is meant to put professionals in touch with what their colleagues are thinking about and doing about new problems; it should help them realize that the intervention process is not a perfect scientific method and that during the process one must often use professional judgment to make difficult but necessary decisions.

Psychiatrists, medical doctors, psychologists, chemical dependence counselors, nurses, social workers, marriage and family therapists, members of the clergy, probation officers, employee assistance counselors, personnel directors, teachers, lawyers, and others can benefit from the basic information provided and from the resources suggested for further training and program development.

PART 1

BASIC CONCEPTS IN INTERVENTION

Introduction*

To understand how intervention works with the problem of chemical dependence, we need to remember that intervention is necessary for many of life's problems:

Tom, a fifty-five-year-old accountant, had been having chest pains for several months. After a thorough assessment, doctors recommended that he have open-heart surgery. Tom told the doctor and his wife not to worry about it, that he'd be all right if he'd just relax a little more and smoke a little less. It was only after the entire family, including several children who flew in from out of state, met with Tom and expressed their concern that they could overcome his denial and get him to accept the recommended treatment.

Allen, a forty-five-year-old executive, was told by his doctor to stop drinking, because it was killing him. His wife, Marsha, told him that she was fed up with his drinking and that he should quit. He'd heard this again and again for years. Finally Marsha sought the help of a counselor. The counselor gave her information, some of which she had never heard, some which she had heard but had ignored or

---

* *Editor's Note:* 1) You'll notice that we've used "alcohol/drugs" throughout this guide as a shortened form of "alcohol or *other* drugs." We've used it because some helping-professionals mistakenly think that alcohol isn't a drug. Of course, it *is* a drug—just as much as cocaine, marijuana, "uppers," "downers," or any other mood-altering substance is. Throughout this guide, we've also used the term "chemical dependence" because it covers dependence on *all* these mood-altering substances and because it's short and simple. 2) To avoid endless repetition of "he or she," we've usually settled for the commoner "he." But keep in mind the real situation: Many women are chemically dependent. For instance, in the United States about 40% of alcoholics are women.

forgotten. The counselor talked to the children as well.

They not only received information; they learned about their personal power and collective strength as a family. They also learned a certain technique that helped them focus their strength on one goal: helping Allen to stop his drinking. The technique: a carefully planned family intervention.

These two cases have a great deal in common. A person faced with a serious illness refuses to believe it. Professional opinions and the input of the spouse are not sufficient. But focused, concerted effort on the part of the entire family finally provides the impetus to overcome the sick person's denial and to get him to accept the treatment he needs.

The fact is, there are many times when we must confront others with uncomfortable facts about what their behavior is doing to us and to others who live or work with them. Although there are similarities among the many types of interventions we do throughout our lives, there are differences as well. The differences depend on the nature of the problem being addressed and the effect the problem has on all those involved.

Intervention with chemical dependence calls for a very special approach. Chemical dependence is an insidious illness that creeps up on a person, confusing and deluding him. What makes it unique, however, is how it can confuse and delude those closest to him as well. It creates a psychological gridlock that keeps chemical dependents and those closest to them locked in self-destructive patterns of feeling, thinking, and acting.

A major role of the professional in family intervention is to loosen up the system of tightly-bound thoughts, feelings, defenses, and behaviors that keep those concerned about a chemically dependent person from taking effective action to help him **and** themselves.

Types or Levels of Intervention

When someone's chemical use is causing problems for himself, his family, his co-workers and others, many things can be done.

Describe the behavior. Those affected by or observing the effects of a chemical dependent's behavior can give the person feedback about how they see him. They can let the person know what he looks like when he's drinking, what he sounds like, what he does, whom he has endangered, and whose feelings he's hurt. "Tom, you've been a special person in my and Ginnie's life. Last night you'd been drinking when you dropped Ginnie off. You may not remember, but you slurred your words, you stumbled when you walked back to the car. It's not like you to place Ginnie in any danger. I don't want you to drive her home anymore when you've been drinking."

Describe your feelings. Concerned relatives, friends, and co-workers can describe the effects the chemical dependent's behavior has on them: how they were hurt, frightened, saddened, angered, or embarrassed by what the person did while under the influence of chemicals. "Betty, I think you're a sophisticated, intelligent woman and most of all a person who respects other people's feelings. You've always been sensitive to others. At the restaurant last night, you had four or five drinks before dinner. I watched how you changed when you were drinking. You became angry at the waitress; nothing was right. I got scared when you kept yelling at her. I get so sad and angry watching alcohol change you. I feel like I'm losing my friend, and I get sad. I even cry sometimes. I want it to be different for us."

Stop protecting the person from the effects of his chemical use. Many of us automatically seek to protect from the consequences of his chemical use a person who is drunk, high, or hung over. We might protect him from physically hurting himself, clean up his messes, lie to his friends and co-workers for him, or give him sympathy instead of honesty and insight. This kind of behavior is called enabling: We "enable" a person to get by with his chemical use without having to deal with the consequences.

Offer the person help for his alcohol/drug problem. Many professional and self-help resources are available to a person suffering from chemical dependence. An important step in any form of intervention is to let the person know where help is available, and specifically how to get that help: "Joe, you and I have been friends for a long time. I worry about what alcohol is doing to your life, and I know you are too, because in the last month you've told me several times you think you're drinking too much on the weekends. The county counseling clinic has information on drinking problems. I've made an appointment for us this Tuesday night at 6:00. Let's go see what they have to offer."

Independent decisions by family members. Those closest to the chemical dependent have to make up their own minds about what they're going to do with their lives, whether or not the person stops using alcohol/drugs. For instance, if an alcoholic's wife feels she can no longer live with him if he continues drinking, she must develop the resolve, not only to communicate this to him, but to keep to her resolution if his behavior doesn't change. If the quality of the chemical dependent's work merits dismissal, his supervisor should make the person aware of this and tell him exactly what improvements are expected. The supervisor must then follow through with that decision, if necessary.

These interventions *do* work. The point is, "interventions" can come in many shapes and sizes, and each of them, taken alone, can be quite effective.

Mike's Weekend Escapade. At a breakfast meeting with some co-workers, Mike mentioned that he'd had a terrible time with his girlfriend over the weekend. He'd gotten drunk and had a very loud argument with her in the lobby of her apartment building at about 2 o'clock Saturday morning. The police were called, but no one was arrested. When Mike said, somewhat shyly, that maybe he should do something about his drinking, all of his friends laughed it off nervously, telling him he didn't have anything to worry about, that he'd just had a bad night. One friend, however, said that maybe Mike did have something to worry about and should go see the employee assistance counselor at the company where they all worked. That was all that was said; but Mike did, in fact, go to see the counselor.

Too Many Apologies. Bill was a chronic alcoholic who had had many years in A.A.—and many slips. It was customary for him, after he'd behaved rudely to his friends while drinking, to call each of them and apologize. He'd invariably say, "You know I wouldn't have done that if I wasn't drinking." Most of the time his friend Joe would say, "I know that, Bill; don't worry about it." This time, however, Joe said something slightly different: "Bill, you and I have been friends for a long time. It's true that when you're drinking you're not fully aware of how alcohol affects you. I've heard you make a number of crude remarks about my wife. I was hurt—deeply. I know you've been in the program struggling, and I know it's hard to choose not to drink. But it's still not O.K. with me when you hurt the feelings of a friend. I want to support you in staying with and working the program." Much, much later, when Bill had more than a year's sobriety behind him, he admitted to Joe that his confrontation, simple and mild though it was, had had a very powerful impact on him.

Many simple, straightforward confrontations can be effective when even one person tries them. They would be even more effective if **everyone** were willing to try them. If every chemical dependent heard, continually and consistently from each of his friends and family members, just how he acted and how they felt when he got drunk or high, the dependents would probably seek help more often and sooner than they usually do.

While these interventions with chemical dependents, done by individuals at different times, **can** and **do** work, **they don't always work reliably**. For example, if an alcoholic hears from his wife that he has a problem, his best friend may later assure him he doesn't. Others may also be very concerned about the alcoholic and confront him but may offer no suggestions for change other than "Just tell yourself you don't need to drink and you won't."

In order to help your clients maximize their chances of getting a chemically dependent person to listen to their concerns and accept the help he needs, you need to use a methodical, carefully planned technique. That technique is known as "structured intervention," "family intervention," or, most often, simply "intervention."

The Five Key Components of an Intervention

The type of intervention discussed in this book was developed by Dr. Vernon E. Johnson, founder of the Johnson Institute, where it was used and found to be highly successful in getting chemically dependent persons to accept treatment for their problem. In his latest book, *Intervention: How to Help Someone Who Doesn't Want Help, A Step-By-Step Guide for Families and Friends of Chemically Dependent Persons,* published by the Johnson Institute, Dr. Johnson shows concerned persons how to use the process and explains the clinical premises upon which it's based.

Intervention was born from a five-year practical research program started by Dr. Johnson in 1962. Frustrated by his and other counselors' inability to get alcoholics to examine and understand the effects their drinking was having on them and on their loved ones, Dr. Johnson distributed a questionnaire to 200 recovering alcoholics. Their responses led to one profound conclusion: **crisis**, rather than spontaneous insight, was the key to recovery.

The study showed that all the clients had experienced a buildup of crises in many areas of their lives and that those crises had been directly related to their drinking. Those crises had **forced** them to recognize and deal with their alcoholism. This led Dr. Johnson and his colleagues to wonder why they had to wait for such crises to occur. Why couldn't they use crises creatively as a basis for intervention?

After attempting a variety of approaches, they found that the most useful one was to bring together concerned relatives and friends of the alcoholic and help them present reality in a receivable way to the alcoholic. By "reality" they meant the facts of the disease: how the alcoholic behaved while intoxicated; specific things he did while under the influence; how the alcoholic's family relationships, job, and health had been affected by the disease, and so on. By "receivable way" they meant that the friends and relatives had to present such facts in an objective, nonjudgmental, caring way.

After some refinement, they discovered that the most effective interventions involved five simple but extremely important steps:

1. **Gather together people who are very meaningful to the chemically dependent person and who are concerned about his alcohol/drug use.** These persons can be spouses, children, other relatives, close friends, ministers, doctors, or employers. These people will need firsthand knowledge of incidents and behavior related to the person's chemical

use, such as blackouts, DWIs (arrests for driving while intoxicated), loss of behavioral control, accidents, personal threats, or injury to self or others.

2. **Have those people make written lists of specific data about the person's alcohol/drug use and its effects as well as their feeling responses.** This must be **firsthand** knowledge of incidents and behavior; gossip and secondhand information should be avoided. Generalities such as "Tom, we all think you're drinking too much" will **not** suffice. The people reporting the data should indicate how that behavior or incident affected them emotionally and how it has affected their relationship with the chemically dependent person. Observations about general changes in the person's character, behavior, and personality can be reported as well, but they should follow the list of specific data about behavior.

The data **must** be reported in a nonjudgmental manner that expresses care and concern for the chemical dependent. Concerned persons must avoid talking down to the person, expressing anger, or being judgmental.

3. **Have the concerned persons decide upon a specific treatment plan that they expect the chemically dependent person to accept.** The concerned persons must decide beforehand what type of help they want the alcoholic to get. This is the critical link in the intervention chain. The goal is not only to get the person to accept the help he needs, but to accept this help **immediately** upon conclusion of the intervention session.

Some counselors who act as professional facilitators for structured interventions are willing to employ "what if" clauses; others aren't. A "what if" clause is used when the person won't accept a recommended course of action without trying it **his way** first. In such cases, the family may say,

"OK, John, you can try your plan. But we want you to agree now that, if your plan doesn't work and you start to drink again, you'll immediately go to Park City Hospital for treatment."

4. **Have the concerned persons decide beforehand what** *they* **will do if the chemically dependent person rejects all forms of help.** A spouse may have to say, "If you won't accept treatment, I can't subject the children or myself to living with your cocaine use any longer." The employer may say, "We aren't recommending your **best** alternative; we're recommending your **only** alternative. I've given you too many chances in the past; this is your last one. If you want your job, you'll go to treatment."

It's not always necessary for concerned others to express their "bottom lines." Quite often, the overwhelming impact of the specific data on the chemical dependent is sufficient to get him not only to accept help but to **want** it.

5. **Meet as a group with the chemically dependent person and present the data and recommendations in an objective, caring, nonjudgmental manner.** A caring and nonjudgmental manner is crucial to the intervention process. Those who can't control their anger at the time of the intervention shouldn't participate. Later, when the chemically dependent person is in treatment, time should be provided for the family and concerned persons to express their anger and to work through it, ideally in a structured family counseling program that the treatment center provides. The structured intervention scene is definitely **not** the appropriate time.

Why Intervention Works

Intervention doesn't work through intimidation and coercion but through care and concern coupled with specific, incontrovertible evidence that moves the person to accept the reality of his condition and accept the help he needs. This form of intervention has been effective because it's very **different** from anything the chemically dependent person has had to face during his years of alcohol/drug use. Let's look at what some of those differences are:

1. **The *sources* of anger and resentment, not the anger and resentment themselves, are expressed.** Some helping-professionals may say it's phoney to express care and concern to chemical dependents when really what the spouses and friends want to do is express their extreme anger, frustration, and resentment to them. But it's simply not effective to express anger and resentment to a chemical dependent **during structured intervention**. Besides, anger is rarely a primary emotion. It's usually a secondary emotion underlying primary feelings such as guilt, shame, hurt, fear, embarrassment, or sadness. Although these primary emotions are commonly shared among helping-professionals and among people who have received counseling or therapy, they're seldom shared by chemical dependents and their families. So when a chemically dependent person walks into a room of family members and friends, he'll most likely be afraid of their anger and of being attacked—he's experienced this before. When the anger or the attack doesn't come, a transformation begins to happen. He's usually so surprised by the fact that anger **isn't** being expressed that he becomes exceptionally open, if only briefly, to hearing what the group of concerned persons has to say.

2. **A *group* of people have assembled out of concern just for him.** The fact is obvious, but the impact of it may not be. How often in our lives do family or friends gather in a group, tell us directly that they love us and are concerned about us, and give us honest information about what we're

doing to ourselves and others? For most people, this simply doesn't happen. This is what makes intervention such a powerful and unique experience. One alcoholic in treatment described how intervention affected him: "I think I knew deep down inside what my drinking was doing to me. I don't think I ever knew or could have known, though, that so many people were genuinely concerned about my drinking. Sure, they were upset about some of the things I'd done that interfered with their lives. But they were mostly concerned about what I was doing to myself. That really shook me."

3. **Specific data, not judgments, opinions, or accusations, is shared.** This is another unique thing about intervention, not for therapists perhaps, but for most people, and certainly for those living with a chemical dependent. People generally filter their perceptions through their own prejudices and experiences. They also base what they say on their personal opinions and judgments. Chemical dependents are well prepared to fight back against general opinions, judgments, or accusations. They're **not** prepared to hear clear, specific facts from persons close to them about their behavior and its effects. Many skeptical counselors have come to believe alcoholics when they say, "I didn't know what drinking was doing to me. I really didn't know."

4. **The structured intervention session is action-oriented, with an immediate behavioral goal.** In this way the intervention session differs from most counseling or psychotherapeutic techniques that professionals are familiar with. The structured intervention session is focused on helping the chemical dependent open up his defenses long enough for him to see what his chemical use is doing to him and others and to see what alternatives are available to him for dealing with the problem **now**. The alcoholic may remain open to what others have said to him for a long time, or until his next

drunk, or until he meets a buddy who's willing to discount the feelings and data presented by the concerned persons during the intervention. It's a short-term focus. It **does** fit smoothly into a long-term process of change, but the structure is built around the immediate goal of getting the person to accept help. The immediacy of the treatment alternative is important here. A **structured intervention** may open a window of opportunity for only a very short time. After a few days or weeks, the impact of all the data and all the concern expressed will begin to fade. Having an action plan ready to go at the moment when the chemical dependent is most open to it is critical.

Please note that the "success" of an intervention isn't determined solely by the response or reaction of the chemically dependent person. As will be made clear later, your client will seldom be the chemically dependent person but rather will be the family member or other concerned person who has come to you for help. If the concerned persons have been able to develop the awareness, courage, and skill to participate in a structured intervention session, that in itself is a therapeutic success. They'll have made major changes in their lives and will have had a strong impact on the chemical dependent whether or not he's able or willing to admit it.

Intervention is a process that interrupts the enabling family system that surrounds a chemically dependent person. The structured intervention session is **just the beginning of the process for the whole family, not a single event for the sole benefit of the chemical dependent**. For that reason, a health care or recovery plan for each family member should be developed so that the process of recovery can continue for everyone after the conclusion of the structured intervention session.

It's an extremely *thorough* approach. All bases are covered. The key people are there, so the chemical dependent is less likely to go to someone else for a second opinion. The presentation is like nothing he has ever heard before, so his usual defenses don't work. A specific plan is ready, so the impact doesn't get diffused in the ensuing weeks. All this comes together at one time. The collective power of the concerned persons has been mobilized, and there's no escape hatch. If any of the crucial ingredients is missing—as often happens when professionals and laypeople try to intervene alone—the intervention is much less likely to be effective.

The Dynamics of Intervention

Several key factors are at work in the intervention process. How these factors interact creates a dynamic tension that makes each intervention unique in how it's planned and carried out. Assessing and working with these factors and the dynamics they create is an important task for the professional. These key factors are:

1. Power
2. Value conflicts
3. Delusion and denial
4. Enabling
5. System-based resistance

1. **Power factors in intervention.** In preparing concerned persons for a structured intervention, a professional counselor must help them realize what power they have and to decide what power they're willing to use. The power to intervene comes in many different forms:

- **The power of loved ones.** When a chemically dependent person realizes that his drinking has been hurting a loved one, that factor alone can be enough to get the person to accept help. This isn't a naive hope. When concerned persons begin the intervention process, they often **presume** that the chemically dependent person is truly aware of what his alcohol/drug related behavior is doing to them, but that presumption is usually incorrect. Although he may have heard some complaints, he probably will have minimized them or rationalized them so that he doesn't fully realize how the persons who complained really felt about his behavior. He'll most likely have forgotten just how many times he's done something hurtful. A structured intervention lays out clearly the cumulative effects of his behavior on loved ones.

Children can have an important part in the intervention process simply because of their ability to tap the parental instincts of the chemically dependent parent. However, because of their extreme vulnerability, their involvement in a structured intervention session can sometimes place an inappropriate and unwarranted emotional burden on them. A professional must critically assess and judge each case in which a child's involvement is being considered.

- **Power related to emotional dependence.** Some chemical dependents aren't entirely swayed by learning that their behavior is hurting family members. This doesn't necessarily indicate a lack of love or commitment to the relationship—although it certainly may. Rather, it may simply indicate the person's inability to accept the fact that his behavior has been so hurtful when he hasn't intended it to be. If the person isn't moved by learning of the effects of his behavior on a family member or friend, he may be moved only by the possibility of losing a relationship on which he depends. Perhaps he's not willing to hear his wife when she describes how he's hurt her, but he may sit up and listen when he hears or senses the possibility that she won't continue to live in a hurtful, co-dependent relationship.* This doesn't always mean leaving the relationship; rather, it may mean changing it and/or building a new relationship that's different: "John, I care deeply about what's happening to us. I'm not going to keep covering up the problems alcohol is causing in our lives. I'll call your boss if you want, but this time I'll say you're too sick from your hangover rather than from the flu. I don't want to protect your drinking anymore. I love you and want things to be different for us. And I want us **all** to get help."

- **The employer's power.** Obviously, if an employer is fed up with a chemical dependent's behavior, this can have a strong effect on the dependent's willingness to accept treatment. The threat of losing job security doesn't have to come from a person with direct supervisory power over an individual. In fact, it may not always be appropriate to have a person's boss involved in an intervention, since some of the material shared there could be very personal. A close friend who works with the chemically dependent person, however, could provide an objective description of the risks the person is facing on the job. That friend could also pledge not to enable the chemical dependent to get through the work day by covering up for him or helping him complete projects when he's too hung over or too shaky to be effective.

---

* The term "co-dependent" refers to those persons who've become psychologically and emotionally dysfunctional as a result of being in a close, dependent relationship with an alcohol/drug dependent person. They tend to be as deluded about the addiction as the chemical dependent himself, and they persist, despite negative consequences, in enabling the chemical dependent to continue his alcohol/drug use. More about co-dependence will follow in the discussion of concerned persons groups in Part 3.

- **Statutory power.** Parents of minors, or close family members willing to sign court commitment papers on their adult chemically dependent relatives, have power that can be exercised if it's necessary and appropriate to do so. Commitment laws vary from state to state and usually are used to force into treatment chemical dependents who are in immediate danger of physically harming themselves or others.

- **Legal power.** Depending on the state law, people who have been convicted of drunk driving or other alcohol/ drug related crimes have forfeited some of their rights to self-determination and may be required to accept treatment for chemical dependence. This kind of power lies in the hands of judges, probation officers, prosecutors, and other professionals in law enforcement, court services, and corrections.

Many concerned persons are unable to recognize their own power because they've developed such deeply ingrained co-dependent traits or even full-blown co-dependent personality disorders. Other concerned persons can become so enmeshed in patterns of denial, delusion, and enabling that their obscured vision keeps them from seeing or using the power available to them. In other instances, concerned persons may feel that the power they have is counterbalanced by power held by the chemical dependent. For example, an alcoholic may be emotionally dependent on his spouse, but the spouse feels financially dependent on the alcoholic. "If I confront him about his drinking, he'll leave me. I wouldn't know what to do. I don't have any job skills, and he'd probably be able to take the kids away from me."

This is why **empowerment** is so important for concerned persons and is a major goal of any professional counseling they receive as part of the intervention process. Empowerment is really claiming health for oneself. Concerned persons need to be aware that being able to describe reality **is** power. Health means owning one's own part in the problem and being willing to change.

Power shouldn't be flaunted by concerned persons. It can produce shame and be very counterproductive. A wife doesn't always have to tell her husband she's going to leave if he doesn't stop drinking. He may already have gotten that message by sensing her resolve as she presents her data. A probation officer would much rather have a client see the need for treatment than have the client forced into treatment by order of the court.

Not every bit of power available to interveners should be used. How and when power is used depends on where the value conflicts lie.

2. **Value Conflicts: Internal, or External?** Any type of intervention, including the structured intervention described in this book, works best if the chemically dependent person feels some characterological conflict about his behavior. For instance, if an alcoholic feels some sense of guilt when he hears he has hurt and embarrassed others while under the influence of alcohol, those feelings may motivate him to change. In such cases, the need to apply stronger forms of leverage—threat of job loss, incarceration, or commitment to a treatment unit—may not be necessary.

It's very important for professionals to help clients understand the difference between guilt and shame. Guilt is a necessary, healthy, and powerful feeling that helps people set boundaries that protect them from their own excesses. Guilt gives people "a way back," a way to heal wrong through restitution. The purpose of feeling guilt is to change. Shame, on the other hand, is a feeling that causes people to feel they're bad persons. Shame-based statements such as "only an idiot or crazy person would do what you did" or questions such as "how could you have done such a stupid thing?" attack the person and give him no way back. Persons who've repeatedly been shamed begin to believe they're not responsible, that life just happens to them, that they're victims.

Many chemically dependent persons, adults and teenagers alike, don't experience characterological or internal conflicts. Sometimes teenage alcohol/drug abusers are involved with a peer group that views chemical use as the norm. They really don't feel any conflict about it. Since the chemical use conflicts only with their parents' and/or the community's values, the parents and other representatives of the community (e.g., teachers, law enforcement officials) must exercise some form of external power and control. This creates an external value conflict for the teenager who uses chemicals. If an adult has a history of psychopathic behavior in addition to chemical dependence, external control in the form of threats of commitment or incarceration may also be necessary. Internal value conflicts create feelings of discomfort that have their source within the chemically dependent person himself. External value conflicts create feelings of discomfort in the people who are affected by the chemically dependent person's behavior. Such persons seek relief from the feelings of discomfort by focusing the need for change on the chemically dependent person.

As value conflicts move from being internal to being external, the source of power also moves from internal to external. If there's no internal, characterological conflict for the chemically dependent person, but a considerable amount of external conflict for family members, the family will have to use all the power and leverage available to it. Sometimes, if family systems are extremely rigid, conflicts may be external not only to the dependent but to the family as well. An example would be if one member of a family goes to jail on a second DWI charge and the other family members respond by viewing the incident as just another instance of "police harassment." When there's no clear conflict of values, either internal or external, within the family, then even though an adult or teenage family member is in serious trouble with chemical dependence, the power to intervene may have to come from outside the family. Child-protection services may have to pressure the parents of a chemically dependent adolescent; or a judge may have to pressure an alcoholic convicted of drunk-driving into accepting treatment. Unfortunately, this focus actually gives the power to the chemically dependent person and creates only fear in other family members. Intervention in the best sense of the term is a process that allows family members to focus on their own internal value system, share this value system with the chemically dependent person, and encourage a journey together whereby each family member gets help.

3. **Delusion and denial.** Delusion and denial are two of the foundation stones of chemical dependence. Long after serious consequences start affecting an alcoholic, his family, his friends, his driving ability, and his job, delusion and denial will still strongly support his continuing to drink.

Delusion refers to all those dynamics characteristic of chemical dependence that help an alcohol/drug dependent person continue to believe things are really all right; that he's doing a great job; that everyone at the party thought he was outrageously funny; that his kids are doing just fine even though he tends to be a bit moody and unreliable at times. Denial is the inability to accept and deal with the reality of the hurt and pain that alcohol/drug abuse is causing; an inability to see what's there to be seen.

A well-dressed, sophisticated, wealthy fifty-five-year-old woman was sitting in the county attorney's office. She was looking at a video tape made by the State Police who had picked her up for drunk driving. The video tape clearly showed the woman staggering as she attempted to walk a straight line and fumbling as she attempted to touch her finger to her nose. The audio portion of the tape indicated that she was slurring her words and couldn't complete a coherent sentence. As she watched the video tape, she repeated, clearly and confidently, "That's not me. That is not me!"

The sources of delusion and denial are many:

- **Blackouts.** Blackouts are chemically induced periods of amnesia in which experiences are not transferred from short-term to long-term memory. During a blackout, a person is conscious and can, in fact, be quite animated. Blackouts are very real psycho-physiological phenomena and are not based on emotional problems. A blackout is often confused with passing out. The two aren't the same, however, even though a drinker can pass out **during** a blackout. Passing out means unconsciousness: The drinker appears to fall asleep abruptly. A blackout is different and usually has nothing to do with falling asleep. It's amnesia: a period of seconds, minutes, hours, or even days during which the drinker is awake and active but later remembers nothing about the events that took place. Many alcoholics have awakened in the morning, filled with terror about what might have happened the night before. They may not have remembered driving home and will run down in the morning to look at the car to make sure there hasn't been an accident. Many alcoholics actually tell of looking for blood on the bumpers to make sure they haven't hit anyone while driving home drunk and in a blackout.

- **Repression.** This is the process by which unacceptable feelings and memories are buried deep in a person's unconscious. Thoughts that are repressed aren't available to the chemical dependent's consciousness. The more painful the memory, the more it conflicts with his values, the more likely it is to be repressed. When an alcoholic is told during an intervention that one night while intoxicated he made a pass at the babysitter while driving her home, his shock may be genuine, his shame very real.

- **Euphoric recall.** This is the tendency of chemical dependents to remember only the good times and the good feelings they had when they were drunk or high. It's usually accompanied by the tendency to view one's performance while intoxicated as being exceptional when in fact the actual performance—musical, professional, physical—was poor and often inappropriate. The morning after a big party, an alcoholic might come downstairs chuckling to himself and remind his wife of his hilarious antics of the previous night. She might well be in tears because she was so embarrassed that he had offended the hostess, spilled food and drinks all over the couch, and told obscene jokes to anyone who'd listen.

- **Rationalization.** This refers to the ways in which we humans can find "rational," plausible explanations and excuses for our unacceptable behavior. We invent excuses so as to make unacceptable behavior seem acceptable. "Let's see. That meeting doesn't start until 1:30, and there's no use in my going back to the office just to shuffle some papers. I think I'll have another drink—or two—just to calm my nerves." "If I get too nervous and blow my presentation, I'll be in deep trouble. A couple of drinks beforehand will probably be good for both me and the company."

- **Justifying, excusing, and blaming.** These behaviors are all means of seeking external reasons for using alcohol/drugs and for the problems related to that chemical use. "If Tom hadn't been late meeting me for lunch, I wouldn't have had those extra drinks." "A man only gets out of town once in a while; it doesn't hurt to tie one on at a convention." "If you had kids [or a wife or husband or job] like I have, you'd drink too."

- **Intellectualizing.** Some people don't seek personal excuses for their alcohol/drug use but rather seek complex psycho-social factors that explain it or lead to it. "Some of the best poets of our time did their best work only when they were drunk." "Coleridge used opium; I'm a writer, so why shouldn't I use coke?" "I'm a sensitive, artistic person who feels too strongly the pressures of society. Smoking pot mellows me out so I can stand it."

- **Minimizing.** Minimizing is the process by which a person attempts to make something appear less serious than it is. "I may have had a few drinks, but that's nothing to get upset about." "Hey, so we had a close call last night. I knew what I was doing all the time. That truck was a good ten feet away from us."

- **Compensating.** A person can do poorly on his job for three or four weeks and then, by putting in an exceptional effort just before a report is due, still appear to be doing acceptable work. The ability to compensate for hung-over or strung-out periods keeps the chemically dependent person believing there's no problem: "Boy, that's one hell of a report I produced. And they talk about me having a drinking problem, huh? This'll put those concerns to rest once and for all."

Although we've emphasized here how delusion and denial are exhibited in the behavior of chemically dependent persons, it's important to note that concerned persons and even helping-professionals themselves can also engage in many of these behaviors.

Delusion and denial weave themselves so deeply into the family life of a chemically dependent person that it's difficult for a professional working with that family to untangle the web. Delusion and denial also work to push the chemical dependent deeper and deeper into the disease process. Then, the truth about a chemical dependent's alcohol/drug use becomes literally inaccessible to him unless it's brought back powerfully and concretely through the intervention process.

Spouses seem particularly vulnerable to being caught up in the web of denial and delusion. Many simply accept the chemical dependent's version of reality rather than trusting their own perception of what's happening.

The many ways in which spouses and others tend to take care of and protect chemical dependents from the effects of their chemical use also contribute to delusion and denial. "If he can drink heavily and still get to work, things can't be so bad." The fact that his wife always has to wake him up, shake him out of bed, and help him get showered and dressed doesn't seem to matter. The fact that she also feels compelled to keep him from having one too many at parties or other social gatherings doesn't seem to register either. If he still has the job, things must be all right. This protecting and shielding is called **enabling**, a key dynamic in the development of chemical dependence and one that must be addressed for intervention to proceed.

4. **Enabling.** Enabling is a natural, inevitable concomitant of chemical dependence, and you should encourage your clients to let go of their feelings of guilt for having engaged in enabling behaviors. However, helping-professionals should help their clients become aware of **how** they're enabling and encourage them to stop that behavior. Enabling refers to

those reactions or behaviors of family members, friends, employers, or co-workers of a chemical dependent that shield him from experiencing the harmful consequences of his alcohol/drug use. Many of the little things done out of love, concern, or fear for an alcoholic only help that person avoid the pain, embarrassment, and guilt that he **needs** to feel if he's ever to develop the motivation to change.

Spouses enable by:

- Changing their lifestyles to accommodate the drinking habits of an alcoholic: e.g., going along with his refusal to attend social functions where alcohol isn't served, trying desperately to avoid all functions at which alcohol is served.

- Disposing of alcohol/drugs so the chemical dependent won't have access to them.

- Keeping up appearances, such as making sure the chemical dependent gets a haircut or is clean, neat, and properly dressed.

- Being responsible for waking him, especially when he's hung over, so he'll get to work.

- Doing all the household chores that are his responsibility.

- Taking care of the alcoholic when he's sick from drinking; cleaning up the bed, the floor, or the alcoholic himself when he vomits.

- Consoling the chemical dependent when he's feeling sorry for himself because of problems he's having that are alcohol/drug related.

- Making excuses for the chemical dependent or lying to the employer, relatives, friends and even the children about his behavior.

Co-workers enable by:

- Doing the work of an employee who's impaired by alcohol/drug use; covering up his mistakes or poor performance.
- Joining him or keeping up with him when he's drinking heavily; helping him believe his alcohol/drug use is normal.
- Making excuses for the chemical dependent by emphasizing to the employer or spouse the work pressures he's experiencing.
- Lying to the supervisor about a chemical dependent's brief or prolonged absence during the work day.

Employers enable by:

- Allowing an employee with a consistent pattern of absences or prolonged sick leaves to continue unchecked.
- Relieving an employee with a suspected drinking problem of part of the normal work load, or reassigning him to a less stressful position.
- Continuously excusing an alcohol/drug impaired employee's inappropriate behavior with customers or other employees.

Helping-professionals enable by:

- Making a diagnosis or assessment based solely on the self-report of the chemical dependent.
- Looking at alcohol use as a symptom when it may have developed into the primary disease of alcoholism.
- Focusing therapeutic efforts on discovering the underlying psychological, emotional, or social causes for the alcohol/drug use before treatment.

- Focusing therapeutic efforts on the results of the alcohol/drug use rather then on the chemical use itself. Marriage counselors often fall into this when they try to work on improving communication skills between couples to prevent them from arguing, when in fact most of their arguments happen because one of them is drunk or high.
- Focusing therapeutic efforts on keeping the chemical dependent from feeling guilty when in fact guilt is appropriate. For example, to tell an alcoholic not to be too hard on himself because he let his children down and broke promises is often inappropriate. Chemical dependents need to take a good, hard look at what effects their behavior is having on others and must accept responsibility for those effects.
- Prescribing or suggesting a prescription for tranquilizers or other drugs in order to help the chemical dependent cope with his problems.
- Failing to make it clear that the chemical dependent may not come to a counseling session while under the influence of alcohol/drugs.
- Continuing to counsel a diagnosed alcoholic while the drinking continues; not making abstinence a requirement of ongoing counseling or therapy.

5. **System-based resistance.** The constellation of chemical dependence, denial, delusion, and enabling, while appearing chaotic and purposeless, can in fact be a finely tuned system in which each of the players steadfastly adheres to his or her role in that system. Many clinicians have written about the general pattern of relationships in families with chemical dependence. Despite many variations, they all describe families whose members tend to adopt specific roles and stay

rigidly locked into those roles in order to cope. Their own self-concepts and the expectations of the rest of the family work together to maintain the system's status quo. Some of the rigid roles family members often adopt are:

- **High-achieving children** help convince other family members, especially the parents, that their family is a normal, healthy family despite some problems.
- **Rebellious children** tend to get into trouble and thus serve as a focal point for the family—someone to blame the family's problems on.
- **Humorous, cute, attractive children** can serve to distract the family from its problems by drawing attention to themselves whenever conflict is brewing.
- **Quiet, withdrawn children** tend to avoid creating conflict by withdrawing into their own world. They're somewhat removed from the rest of the family's conscious awareness and often get lost in the struggle.
- **The spouses** of chemical dependents often assume the role of caretaker or martyr in their family systems.

Any of these roles can be assumed by individual family members and can shift over time. For example, a quiet, withdrawn child may gradually or suddenly change and become rebellious, hostile, or even develop serious behavioral problems.

Whatever your perspective on family systems, you've probably learned that those systems aren't easily changed. A key role for the professional in intervention is to help the family system become open enough to accept the changes called for by the intervention process. If the chemical dependent does accept help, the professional should also be available to help the family adjust to the changes they must go through (many of them difficult) when the chemical dependent **stops** drinking/using.

PART 2

THE ROLE OF THE PROFESSIONAL IN INTERVENTION

Introduction

A professional can do many things to facilitate the process of intervention. Before a counselor or therapist gets involved in intervention for chemical dependence, he or she must first have a clear perception of who the actual client is.

Who is the client? In a contractual relationship, the client is usually the person who comes to you requesting service. When you're facilitating interventions with chemical dependence, the client is seldom going to be the alcohol/drug dependent person. Rather, you'll be facilitating the intervention with **the concerned persons,** and **they are your actual clients**.

The point may be obvious, but it's easy to lose track of this fact as work progresses on intervention planning. The success of the intervention hinges not only on how well the chemical dependent reacts, but also on **how well prepared the concerned persons are and how able they've become to make their own decisions**.

There **are** instances in which the chemically dependent person may actually be your client in an intervention process. If you're providing counseling or therapy to someone, you may get cues that alcohol/drugs are causing problems for this person and for those who live or work with him. If the self-report of the client concerning his chemical use seems guarded and incomplete, you can ask permission to talk to his wife and family. If evidence starts to accumulate that chemical use is a serious problem, you can ask the spouse and children to prepare lists of data concerning the effects of your client's chemical use, and you can facilitate a session in which they present this data to your client.

There can be a conflict of interest, however, when you become very involved with a client's family without the client's awareness. It's **not** a conflict of interest, when talking to that client's spouse or children, to recommend that they get support for themselves through Al-Anon, or even that they see another counselor who's skilled in facilitating structured interventions.

You should be forthright in telling a chemically dependent client that you've made those kinds of recommendations, then continue to give him the support, insight, and confrontation he needs in order to make changes. You might also have to say that there's no point in continuing the counseling or therapeutic process unless he gets help for his chemical use problem.

By doing all of this, you'll have played a very important, professionally responsible role in the intervention process, even though you haven't guided the concerned persons through the complete process of a structured intervention.

Who does interventions? Another basic premise to keep clearly in mind when you attempt to clarify your role in the intervention process is this: **As professionals, we don't do the intervening.** Rather:

Spouses intervene.

Children intervene.

Relatives and friends intervene.

Employers intervene.

Colleagues intervene.

Probation officers intervene.

These are the people who provide the data, deliver the data, decide what **they'll** do whether or not the chemical dependent agrees to make the recommended changes, and provide the power and caring needed to make the intervention work. However, the helping-professional's ongoing facilitation and support of all these processes is very important.

A warning about the "Super Counselor Syndrome." We helping-professionals aren't always immune to grandiose behavior, and some of us occasionally try to assume power not rightfully ours. Instead of relying on specific data and the power of meaningful people, we might tend to rely on our own charisma, our own knowledge and experience with chemical dependence, and especially on our own counseling expertise. When this happens, the presentation of data from concerned persons often takes a back seat and the counselor assumes an aggressive, confrontational approach in an attempt to badger the chemical dependent into treatment. **This is not intervention** as we're describing it. It's confrontation only, and very often it backfires—to the regret of all concerned.

Some concerned persons **do** carry out intervention on their own without the help of professionals. However, experience has shown that because of the intense emotional involvement or disturbance shown by some or all of the concerned persons, it's easy for them to lose the focus during an actual intervention session. The Johnson Institute has developed both printed and audiovisual materials to help family members and other concerned persons prepare for the task.* But a primary goal of the Johnson Institute has been to educate and train helping-professionals to become active and effective facilitators of the intervention process, which involves helping families to become ready and able to proceed. To that end the Johnson Institute continues to provide a variety of Professional Intervention Training Seminars in major cities throughout the United States and abroad.** A number of organizations provide information about how to intervene with professionals who work in specific occupations such as medicine, dentistry, law, and piloting.

---

* See Part 5, Further Resources for Programming, for a list of appropriate self-help materials.

** For more information about Johnson Institute Professional Intervention and other Training Seminars, write the Director of Training, Johnson Institute, 510 First Avenue North, Minneapolis, MN 55403, or call 1-800-231-5165; in Minnesota, call 1-800-247-0484.

Intervention is **not** a mysterious concept. The basic steps are clear and simple. This doesn't mean that intervention is easy to do, however. Each one of the steps can be misunderstood or misapplied unless a concerned, competent professional is giving guidance. This is where you, as the professional, come into the picture.

Basically, your role as a professional in facilitating the intervention process is to:

1. **Assess the client's situation** and extenuating circumstances, using the information provided by concerned persons.

2. **Educate the concerned persons** about the disease of chemical dependence and its effects on the chemically dependent person and on those living or working with that person; encourage them to attend Al-Anon.

3. **Provide information** about the intervention process and available treatment services.

4. **Provide counseling and support.**

5. **Prepare the concerned persons** to do the intervention.

6. **Facilitate the intervention session.**

7. **Help the concerned persons to process the results** of the structured intervention session and to make decisions about what they will do with their lives regardless of the outcome.

A professional counselor/therapist may perform one or all of these functions in facilitating the intervention process.

But again, the people who have legitimate personal, legal, or financial power are those who actually do the intervention. Counselors and therapists simply prepare them adequately to do an intervention so that it's helpful to all concerned. A properly prepared intervention will usually be successful, even if the chemically dependent person doesn't go directly to treatment or stop using chemicals. Proper intervention preparation lays the groundwork for future interventions. Dr. Vernon Johnson encourages all helping-professionals and concerned persons to keep trying, because **intervention is a process, not a single event**. If the first attempt at structured intervention doesn't move the chemically dependent person to accept treatment right away, he'll still be profoundly affected. In time either the shared concern and data will sink in or the alcohol/drug related crises will continue to accumulate to the point where he'll have to do something about his problem. And if concerned persons take the trouble to gather again and present their data in an objective, nonjudgmental, caring fashion, they'll most often succeed in getting that chemically dependent person into treatment.

Even if the chemical dependent doesn't go to treatment, the participation of concerned persons in the process of intervention usually loosens up rigid, enabling family systems and allows each person in the family to choose to grow and develop independently. The family members will usually need assistance from the professional in making decisions about their own health and recovery.

The Professional's Role in Assessment

Regarding assessment, the professional should:

1. Help clients make a preliminary assessment of the effects a chemical dependent's alcohol/drug use is having on all concerned.
2. Help clients look at their own use of chemicals.
3. Help clients determine where the value conflicts lie.
4. Help clients assess their own strengths and weaknesses for participating in the intervention process.
5. Help clients assess the power factors involved.

Helping clients make a preliminary assessment of the effects of alcohol/drug use. The term *preliminary assessment* is used here to emphasize that a definitive diagnosis of chemical dependence can't be made solely on the basis of data provided by the concerned persons.

Keep that clearly in mind. The professional working with a concerned person is **not** in a position to make a diagnosis. The professional **is**, however, in a very good position to encourage the concerned persons to come up with specific data and to help the concerned persons step back and look at that data.

During an intervention session, it's normal for the person with the alcohol/drug problem to challenge the concerned persons about labels: "Are you saying I'm an alcoholic?" Unless a previous intervention has confirmed a diagnosis of alcoholism, the professional or concerned persons should say, "Alcohol has been playing a very negative role in all our lives. We **do** know that your drinking is causing you and us some very difficult problems. We want us **all** to go to treatment. Each of us is going to take a look at our own part. We're asking you to join us by going to treatment for an evaluation. Your first week there will be devoted to evaluation. We want us **all** to get help, and this is a beginning."

While the information provided by concerned persons alone won't confirm a diagnosis, it will be a major contributor to the diagnostic process. It's axiomatic in the field of chemical dependence that if you want to find out what a person's chemical use is **really** like, don't talk to only that person; talk to the person's spouse and other family members whenever possible.

As the intervention process proceeds, the data contributed by concerned persons and from other various sources will usually be mutually reinforcing and will help to build a clear picture that chemical use is a critical problem that must be addressed. If the credibility of key concerned persons begins to seem questionable, that matter must be dealt with immediately. For example, if a couple is getting divorced and a custody battle is pending, this can preclude effective intervention for the time being. Intervention under these circumstances shouldn't be attempted by a spouse who's also the legal adversary of the chemically dependent person.

In addition to asking concerned persons to provide information about the effects of a chemical dependent's alcohol/drug use, the professional counselor may also want to know if they have information as to whether the chemical dependent manifests any of the **eight warning signs of chemical dependence:**

1. **Preoccupation:** Does the person look forward to getting his next drink/pill/fix; plan his day around when and how to get the alcohol/drugs; talk constantly about drinking or getting high?

2. **Gulping drinks, "rushing the high"—taking more alcohol/drugs to start off with:** Does the person take a few quick belts in order to get that cozy feeling he's looking for?

3. **Increased tolerance:** Does it take more alcohol/drugs now to get the person drunk or high than it used to?

4. **Hidden supply:** Does the person keep his bottle or other drug supply in secret places so he can drink or use during the day without anyone's knowing?

5. **Medicinal drinking/drug use:** Does the person use alcohol/drugs to mask pain and deal with fear and other uncomfortable emotions?

6. **Blackouts:** Has the person ever had blackouts? How many? How often?

7. **Using more than intended:** For example, does the person frequently stop off at a bar to have just one drink and end up staying until closing time?

8. **Using alone:** Does the person no longer drink or smoke a joint to be sociable but instead drink or use alone with the main goal to get drunk or high?

Professionals can use other tools to perform a preliminary assessment of a drinking/drug problem. One example is the **Michigan Alcohol Screening Test (MAST)**. The MAST is a brief questionnaire used to diagnose alcoholism. Some chemical dependence counselors think that the MAST may be too obvious—that it makes it easy for a person whose drinking is at issue to take the test. However, they find that when they also have the **spouses** of problem drinkers respond to the test, a clearer, more reliable picture of the degree of alcohol abuse is presented.

Another widely used assessment tool is the **McAndrews Subscale of the Minnesota Multiphasic Personality Inventory (MMPI)**. It's widely used by professionals and is clinically a sounder instrument.

Another preliminary assessment tool often used is the **Children of Alcoholics Screening Test (CAST)**. The CAST is a thirty-question test that investigates the many problems that children may have in living with a problem drinker or alcoholic. In addition to helping children become aware of the problems they're experiencing, it's been used to confront problem drinkers with the effects their drinking is having on their family life. When the children's test results are presented, the data can be very persuasive for convincing problem drinkers that they may be alcoholic and should accept treatment.

Remember that this type of assessment isn't sufficient for diagnosis and therefore won't be acceptable for third-party reimbursement purposes. In the past, some treatment centers devoted the first one or two weeks of their treatment program specifically to "assessment." This would involve a very general assessment process during which the client participated in groups and attended lectures in between sessions with the counselor and doctors who gradually accumulated enough data to make a diagnosis. Treatment centers are now required to have much more efficient assessment procedures. In fact, some third-party payers insist that a diagnosis be made within three days of the client's entering treatment. When a client is referred to treatment on the basis of a preliminary assessment rather than of a diagnosis, the treatment center must act quickly to accumulate sufficient data to do a complete assessment/diagnosis of the chemical use problem.

A warning: No matter how serious the chemical use problem appears to be, a counselor facilitating an intervention must never give the message to concerned persons that **all** the problems they're facing with a chemical dependent are due to the alcohol/drug use. This is especially important in cases where child abuse has occurred. The reason is that, while chemical dependents are usually more abusive when drinking/using, they may **continue to be abusive** even after the chemical use has stopped. It creates false hopes when concerned persons believe that **all their problems will be solved** if the alcohol/drug use stops.

It's not unreasonable, however, to suggest that none or few of their problems **can** be solved **until** the chemical use does stop. Even if chemical dependence isn't the cause of some problems, it will certainly interfere with attempts to solve them.

Helping clients look at their own use of chemicals. It's not uncommon for some family members or other concerned persons to have problems with chemicals. If there are indications that a concerned person has a problem with alcohol/drugs, the counselor must decide whether the intervention process can proceed before that issue is addressed. In many cases both a husband and his wife were admitted for treatment at the same time.

Not all chemical dependents are in the same stage of alcohol/drug dependence. For example, a wife who has a drinking problem herself can be sincerely and deeply concerned about an alcoholic husband who's having frequent blackouts, drives dangerously, and occasionally experiences seizures or delirium tremens. In cases like this, it's appropriate for the counselor to focus on the person with the more severe drinking problem. Furthermore, if the spouse with the more severe drinking problem does accept treatment, the other spouse will generally have to be involved. That probability in itself may be the catalyst that helps the person recognize the problem and accept help.

Helping clients determine where the conflicts lie. If the chemical dependent would probably feel very guilty or feel conflict over causing problems for others, that can alert the counselor as to how much additional leverage will be needed in order to conduct the intervention. If the chemical dependent has a history of acting-out or of sociopathic or psychopathic behavior, that can also alert the counselor that an intervention may not succeed without some additional leverage provided by a probation officer or an employer. If the alcohol/drug-dependent person isn't really concerned about the effects his behavior has on others, then this type of intervention won't be effective and shouldn't be attempted. In a case where there's ongoing spousal and/or child abuse, the resources of a woman's shelter and special intervention programs for men who batter may be the place to begin the process of intervention for chemical dependence.

Helping clients assess their own strengths and weaknesses for intervention. The counseling professional has to estimate each concerned person's ability to recognize problems related to chemical dependence and to follow through on the tasks that must be done if the intervention is to succeed. It may be that the spouse of an alcoholic is so deeply enmeshed in delusion and enabling that he or she is emotionally and intellectually paralyzed. If this is the case, further counseling, therapy, participation in a support group or self-help group may be necessary before the person can develop the stability and strength to actually consider a structured intervention. The "concerned persons groups," described later, are one way to help the spouses of chemically dependent persons develop the ability and strength to carry out an effective intervention.

Helping clients assess the power factors involved. The counselor must assess what power the chemical dependent has, and what power and influence the concerned persons have as individuals and as a group:

- Is the chemical dependent highly invested in his family, in his job, in staying married, in his personal reputation?
- Are the concerned persons feeling extremely dependent—financially or otherwise—on the person they're intervening with? What risks are they willing to take regarding that dependence?
- What relevant legal issues can the concerned persons use with the chemically dependent person (probation, parole, commitment)?
- Is the group of concerned persons influential or powerful enough, or has it become clear that they'll need the leverage of a favored son or daughter or of a friend who's very important to the chemical dependent?

In addition to assessing these power factors, the counselor can help make people realize that certain kinds of power are theirs to use. People are often reluctant to recognize and use the power legitimately available to them. Sometimes some brief assertiveness training techniques will work well to get people prepared to use their power appropriately.

Remember that **assessment of the problem will take the concerned persons only so far.** Although a counseling-professional can't make a definitive diagnosis of alcoholism/drug dependence without meeting directly with the chemically dependent person, sometimes the evidence provided by concerned others is so overwhelming that chemical dependence is clearly the problem. When a spouse reports that her husband has had four drunk-driving arrests in the last two years; has been drunk all weekend every week for the last five years; has been to Alcoholics Anonymous several times but dropped out each time; has been hiding a bottle around the house for the past fifteen years, then the problem seems obvious. If the credibility of the concerned persons isn't in question and their data is not contradictory, someone outside of the family may see quite clearly that alcoholism is a problem for this family.

The concerned persons may not see it that way, however. They may feel the pain but think that somehow it's their fault. They may see the excessive drinking but think it's just the job-related stress that's causing it. They may feel certain that the chemically dependent person has a drinking problem but may rationalize that it's just a bad habit that he could stop if he really wanted to.

When concerned persons feel and think that way, it's unlikely that additional data about their **own** situation is going to convince them to think or feel otherwise. What they need is some education about chemical dependence and what can be done about it.

The Professional's Role in Education

Concerned persons are usually struggling under a heavy load of misinformation. They may presume that a person's ten years of heavy drinking are due to a stressful job. They may presume that if they're just nice enough to the person, he'll recover.

A major role for a professional, then, is to educate the concerned persons about:

1. The disease concept of alcoholism/drug dependence and how the dependence progresses.
2. How the disease has affected the lives of family members.
3. How delusion, denial, and enabling encourage the disease to get worse.
4. The basic principles of intervention.

The goal of these educational sessions with clients is threefold: new knowledge, attitudinal change, behavioral change.

There's an abundance of material written about the disease concept of chemical dependence, delusion, and denial, and the way that enablers help keep the chemical dependent from making necessary changes. For a list of relevant literature, see Part 5, "Further Resources for Programming."

The film "I'll Quit Tomorrow," produced by the Johnson Institute, portrays the disease process and the role that feelings play in it. It also portrays intervention and some of the processes involved in treatment and recovery.

Two other Johnson Institute films, "The Enablers" and "The Intervention," portray in more explicit detail the dynamics of enabling and how structured intervention works.

Dr. Vernon Johnson's book *Intervention: How to Help Someone Who Doesn't Want Help* can also help clients because it's written in simple language and provides a clear, succinct overview of chemical dependence and the intervention process.

The importance of the disease concept in intervention. In 1956 the American Medical Association defined alcoholism as a disease: a deviation from a state of health with a describable train of symptoms. Whether or not you fully agree with the disease concept of alcoholism/chemical dependence, keep in mind the beneficial effects this concept has on the intervention process.

- It keeps chemical dependence out of the realm of moral issues—for which someone might be condemned, demeaned, or looked down upon—and makes it a problem that can be addressed within a medical, mental health, or social service framework. Don't underestimate how important this can be to some of your clients. Some people still consider alcoholism a sign of moral weakness. This concept evokes shame and often leads to emotional paralysis.
- It lets the family members know that they didn't cause the

disease. This is extremely important for the parents, children, spouses, and siblings of alcoholics. You may be surprised to learn how many people think **they** are the cause of their family member's alcohol/drug use.

- Family members, other concerned persons, and even chemical dependents themselves feel hope when they learn there are treatment facilities and many other services available for this recognizable disease.

It's not very important for your clients to know whether chemical dependence should technically be called a disease or whether their spouse, friend, or employee fulfills every criterion established for the disease diagnosis. What **is** important is that they learn to recognize and accept a problem that has been recognized and accepted by others, that has been experienced by others and successfully addressed by others. Family members need to learn that **they're not alone.** This fact empowers them and helps them let go of the guilt and shame that have kept them stuck in their pain. And understanding the disease concept and the surrounding family issues breaks down the isolation of family members and builds hope—the hope that things can be different.

The Professional's Role in Providing Information on Services

People who are locked into a pattern of behavior caused by chemical dependence in their families, or among their friends or co-workers, often feel that little can be done to change the situation. They already know that people have tried to help the chemically dependent person, that he has gone to Alcoholics Anonymous, or that he has spent some time in jail for a DWI offense and "nothing has worked."

Concerned persons who feel that way have to learn that structured intervention and treatment for chemical dependence is tailor-made for the problems they're facing. They must learn that many people living or working with a chemically dependent person have tried a lot of one-on-one or isolated interventions that have been ineffective, but that those who try a structured intervention followed by a treatment program have seen amazing changes in their lives.

In addition to describing the general process and effectiveness of services available for alcohol/drug problems, the professional facilitating an intervention should be able to provide **specific information** about how to contact the key people at various treatment centers. People who are anxious tend to do things to make their situation even more stressful. They might call a treatment center and immediately start telling their life story to the operator. But a counselor facilitating an intervention can tell the spouse what number to call, whom or what service to ask for, and what information to provide. The person who's going to make the call can also be prepared to handle some possible problems. For instance, if a bed isn't immediately available, the concerned person can be instructed to ask when it will be, how one can be reserved, and how he or she will be informed when the bed becomes available. This kind of preliminary instruction helps reduce anxiety and stress and also commits the concerned persons to following through with the entire intervention process.

The Professional's Role in Providing Counseling and Support

Concerned persons, especially family members, may need a considerable amount of counseling and support as they go about preparing for an intervention. Sometimes they can work very quickly through the process and can intervene effectively in only two or three weeks. Others families may be so fearful or so dysfunctional that they won't be able or ready to try intervention for months. The professional can provide the counseling or therapy directly or can recommend appropriate services to the client.

Al-Anon should be recommended to all families and friends of chemical dependents, and especially to those who are considering doing an intervention. However, clients should be given some guidance as they go about choosing a group. They need to be aware that not all Al-Anon groups are alike and that some may not suit them. They should be encouraged to try more than one group and to find someone to process their experiences with, such as a good Al-Anon sponsor. Most important, they should be made aware that Al-Anon isn't a place to go to help the chemical dependent but is a fellowship of persons closely related to chemical dependents who are dedicated to helping **themselves** grow mentally, emotionally, and spiritually.

The Professional's Role in Preparing for the Intervention Session

In preparing for an intervention, the professional involved has four major tasks:

1. To help select and screen meaningful, concerned persons for participation in the intervention session.
2. To help participants in the intervention session to collect and prepare their data.
3. To assure that a treatment alternative has been chosen and is ready.
4. To guide concerned persons through an intervention role-play.

Helping clients select and screen meaningful, concerned persons. "Meaningful, concerned persons" are those who **should** be involved in the intervention for any or all of the following reasons:

- They're directly affected by the chemical use and have personal credibility and leverage with the chemically dependent person: for instance, family members, close friends, employers, or co-workers.

- They've been in a good position to observe the effects of the chemical use on the family. Often a relative outside the immediate family can provide insights and perspective not available either to those in the immediate family or to those completely outside the extended family. A caring, concerned uncle or aunt has frequently played a major role both in supporting concerned persons in their observations and in helping the chemical dependent to hear and accept the data being presented.

- They're people whom the problem drinker likes, loves, respects, feels close to, or is dependent on.

- They have specific leverage with the chemically dependent person: legal, financial, or occupational. For example, employers, supervisors, co-workers, and probation officers can provide this type of leverage.

When a client makes a list of meaningful persons, the counselor can help in reviewing the list. Is it complete? Are there some key people who, if they're not involved in the intervention—**and** in the important educational process that goes along with it—will sabotage efforts to intervene? Are there people on the list who are too angry, too frightened, or who are chemically dependent themselves, and who therefore shouldn't be involved at this time? An alcoholic's best friend, for instance, would be appropriate **if** that friend doesn't also have a drinking/drug problem and is willing to confront the alcoholic about his problem. Sometimes, though, problem drinkers can be effective interveners. The involvement of such persons requires careful assessment, judgment, and guidance from the professional.

Gathering meaningful people together for an intervention can be difficult. Often they live far apart and have widely varying degrees of interest or investment in the problem. A counselor's involvement in the process of forming an intervention group can be very effective. If a concerned spouse calls up friends and relatives and asks them to gather to talk about intervention and how to do it, some of these meaningful persons can become uneasy and hesitant. After one or two meetings, the groups may easily fall apart.

If on the other hand you, as a professional, are available with a structured program for helping concerned persons understand the problem of chemical dependence and the very important role they can play in halting its progression, you can be the rallying point for the group. A concerned spouse doesn't have to call people and ask them to take part in an intervention. Rather, he or she can simply ask others to come to one session to talk with a counselor. That's all. Having a professional explain to the group the importance of intervention and the success this process has had with others may be enough to get them to come to another meeting.

Helping meaningful persons prepare their data. Data for an intervention can be broken down into three basic categories:

- **Specific incidents** in which alcohol/drug use caused fear, hurt, embarrassment, danger, injury, or other negative consequences.
- **Progressive changes in chemical use patterns over time:** how the person now uses more alcohol/drugs than previously; drinks faster or uses more frequently; hides his bottle/drugs, can't stop, or is constantly drunk or high.
- **General changes in health and behavior** over the years, such as weight loss or gain, chronic insomnia, blackouts, frequent absences or sick leave for hangovers or

drinking/using binges, lack of exercise, loss of appetite, weakness, inertia, gastrointestinal problems, impotency or impaired sexual performance. Data presented in this area won't be effective unless it's specific. However, if enough solid, specific information about general health and behavior has been presented, simple statements of concern about the general health and behavior of the problem drinker/drug user presented by a credible, meaningful person can be very effective.

In order to get all the data presented, encourage your clients to do the following:

1. **Be descriptive:** How did the alcohol/drug dependent person look? How did he or she behave? Exactly when did the event happen? Who was there?

2. **Tie specific events directly to specific drinking/drug use.** "Joe, last night you came home. You had a can of beer in your hand. It was 2 a.m. You said you'd been out with the guys again at Pete's Bar. Joe, I was so frightened. I didn't know what had happened to you. You had said you'd be home for dinner. Joe, it's not like you. I'm scared I'm losing you to alcohol. I love you and I want it to be different for us."

3. **State personal feelings about alcohol/drug-related events that describe exactly how you were affected.** "Dad, when I was eight years old, you'd leave me alone in the car outside the bar for hours, and I felt scared, lonely, and sad."

"Two weeks ago last Saturday, you said you'd help me with my car. I waited and waited for you, but you never came. I finally got in touch with you on Sunday morning. You said you'd stopped to get a beer at the bar and you'd got home late. You didn't even remember your commitment. That's not like you. I'm scared about what alcohol is doing to us."

"When you got hurt in that car accident after you'd been drinking, I thought you were going to die. I was frightened and scared. You always prided yourself on how good a driver you were. It's hard to see what drinking is doing to you."

"When I need you and the children need you, you're out with your friends using cocaine. It's hard and sad to see what cocaine is doing to our lives."

"When you called me at work, you were slurring your words. You kept repeating yourself. And you were screaming at me. I believe you'd been drinking because that's not how you are."

"Last Christmas at dinner you'd been drinking. Midway through the meal you threw up at the table. I was afraid and then embarrassed. I love you so much. I'm angry at what the drinking is doing to us."

"Joan, we've been friends for a long, long time. The other night I saw you take a couple of valium pills and then you had at least four drinks. You said things to my husband that hurt his and my feelings. I'm sad and scared about what's been happening, and I want us to get help."

"Mom, I stopped bringing friends home because I'd never know whether you'd be drinking. Last summer, when you'd been drinking, I brought Judy over and you screamed obscenities at her—words I'd never heard you say before. I'm afraid of what's happening to us because of the alcohol."

All concerned persons need a **written list** of what they want to say. They actually bring those lists to the intervention session. The intervention is a very stressful event for all participants. Concerned persons can't be expected to remember the data and shouldn't try to present it from memory. Instead, they should hold those lists plainly in sight and read directly from them.

Having written lists prepared for the intervention session is very important.

Preparing written lists for the intervention session is crucial because:

1. It provides a way prior to the intervention session for the facilitator to weed out judgmental, accusatory, or demeaning statements.
2. It promotes commitment of the concerned persons to the intervention process.
3. It keeps concerned persons focused on what they're there for.
4. It shows the chemical dependent the amount of time, care, and commitment the concerned persons have invested in this process.

Collecting and preparing the data. It's therapeutic for family members to collect the data and to learn to ask pertinent questions, but some counselors do much of the data-collecting themselves. They contact employers, doctors, and others about the effects that chemical use is having on the user. This can be a risky practice. Unless a chemically dependent client has signed a release of confidential information, a counselor has no right to contact an employer or a doctor. It may be, however, that a wife already has legitimate access to medical information and employment data: for instance, material that has been sent to the home and that the chemical dependent has seen. In any event, the gathering of data should be left to the family members and concerned persons unless the counselor has a release of confidential information signed by the chemically dependent person who's the client.

Assuring that a treatment program has been chosen and is ready to receive the chemical dependent. Intervention, as we're describing it here, is a powerful tool designed to address serious problems caused by chemical use. It's **not** designed to be used with all people who've had a few embarrassing incidents with alcohol/drugs or who are drinking more than usual while going through a divorce or some other isolated problem. A professional should critically assess whether there's truly a chemical abuse or dependence problem.

The problem drinkers/drug users who are the focus of this type of intervention will, for the most part, already have tried or been encouraged to try many different paths to sobriety or normal drinking. They probably will have gone to some Alcoholics Anonymous, Narcotics Anonymous, or Cocaine Anonymous meetings; they probably will have tried, at the request of their spouses, friends, co-workers, employers, and others, to cut down on their drinking/drug use; they probably will have made many promises not to behave offensively again at family or other social gatherings. In fact, it's better if many of these efforts have already been made before one attempts a carefully planned, structured intervention. This allows the group, including the chemical dependent himself, to rule out those methods now as ineffective and to focus on primary treatment for chemical dependence as the immediate goal of the intervention.

In addition to seeing that treatment arrangements are made, the professional should take care of any other contingencies. This keeps the chemical dependent from being able to invent reasons why he couldn't possibly go to treatment at this time. Some examples of excuses often heard from chemical dependents and some appropriate responses that have been made by concerned persons are:

"But who'll get the kids off to school?" *"Don't worry, I've talked to my boss, and he'll let me come in a half hour late so I can take care of them."*

"But my classes! What's going to happen to my students?" *"That's all taken care of. Sarah will be taking over your English classes, and I'm going to work with your special composition class."*

"But we're right in the middle of a major contract proposal."
"That's not a problem; we've already got that covered."

It's highly recommended that the chosen treatment center clearly and explicitly devote three to six days of the program to **evaluation.** This allows the professional to tell the chemical dependent with legitimacy that although the group may not know for sure that he **is** chemically dependent, there are certainly some serious problems related to his alcohol/drug use. Then the concerned persons can urge, request, and sometimes even insist that he go to treatment for **further evaluation** and agree to follow the recommendations.

Some may think this type of provision too risky—that the chemically dependent person will remember this and ask to leave after the evaluation phase of the program is completed. However, if proper investigation into the treatment center's program has been carefully carried out, that center's evaluation phase will usually be intense and powerful. The amount of information gained, the input of other patients, and the guidance of experienced and professional staff is usually sufficient to remove the defenses that remain even after the intervention and to convince the person he should complete treatment.

In choosing a treatment center it's also highly recommended that the center have the philosophy and steps of Alcoholics Anonymous integrated into its program, have a clearly defined and structured family counseling program, and have an aftercare program for both the patient and other family members. It's also a matter of professional courtesy that the counselor inform the treatment center about the circumstances surrounding the intervention: who was involved, the feeling-level responses of the chemical dependent, family members, and other concerned persons, and what the treatment center staff should expect upon the client's arrival. Many treatment centers aren't prepared to deal effectively with the anger or other feelings of a chemical dependent who has recently been the subject of a structured intervention. Their ability to do so depends on the anticipatory planning, consistent follow-through, and courteous and cooperative communication of the professional facilitating the intervention.

During the post-intervention session, the concerned persons will have the opportunity to process their feelings with the counselor/facilitator. The chemical dependent rarely has this opportunity and often arrives at the treatment center with increasing feelings of anger, resentment, fear, shame, and guilt. If the person doesn't have the opportunity to process these feelings with an informed and sensitive staff person prior to beginning the evaluation and treatment regimen, these unresolved feelings can seriously interfere with the person's progress in treatment and his subsequent recovery.

Why not Alcoholics Anonymous? It's legitimate to ask, "Why make treatment such a major focus of an intervention? If most people attend A.A. after treatment, why not make that your bottom line?" But the issue isn't whether A.A. is more or less effective than treatment. A.A. is extremely effective **for those who remain in the fellowship**. However, receiving primary treatment as well as participating in A.A. will probably improve the chemically dependent person's chances to recover fully. And chemical dependents who've become the focus of a structured intervention by their families will most likely need all the help they can get.

Are "what if" clauses OK? The film "I'll Quit Tomorrow" portrays an intervention with an alcoholic who promises to stay sober on his own instead of going to treatment. The family decides to go along with that as long as he accepts the "what if" clause: "**What if** you don't stay sober?" In this case, the alcoholic agrees to go to treatment if he has another drink.

Some helping-professionals feel that "what ifs" should be left out of the intervention, because they appear to give the chemical dependent a way out from the pressure of the present moment. This is often true, and for that reason the "what ifs" shouldn't in most cases be presented to the client as alternatives. There may be some structured interventions, however, in which a "what if" is the **only alternative** the chemical dependent is willing to accept. The counselor and family will have to consider that possibility beforehand and will have to decide clearly what they'll do in that instance.

In most cases, concerned persons have experienced an alcoholic's broken promises that he would stop drinking. They're not inclined to be disappointed again and aren't likely to be willing to let the alcoholic off the hook. In cases where a person has frequently stopped drinking/using for a time just to get his spouse off his back, a "what if" clause is going to be just another way to delay and dissipate the impact of the intervention session. What's important is that clear decisions have been made beforehand about what the concerned persons will or won't accept, and these decisions must be carried out consistently if intervention is to be effective.

Guiding concerned persons through an intervention role-play. Before the intervention takes place, the professional should assist the concerned persons in a role-play of the intervention. Before the role-play, the group will have to complete a number of steps.

1) Choose a leader. Someone **other than the chemical dependent's spouse** should be chosen to speak for the group. The reason the spouse shouldn't be chosen is that there are usually too many conflicting emotions between the spouse and the chemical dependent. Also, one should avoid having the chemically dependent feel as though all the data has been gathered solely at the urging of the spouse. The chemical dependent should understand clearly that **many independent observations** are being presented by persons who care enough to share their concerns.

While you, as the professional, can lead the session, it's more effective if someone else (such as a close friend) whom the chemical dependent already knows, respects, and finds very credible assumes that role. You can introduce yourself to the chemically dependent person and say that these people have gathered out of concern for him and one another and that they'd like to share what those concerns are. The close friend can then direct the intervention with occasional assistance from you, when necessary.

Make sure the leader knows how to start. Several very important things need to be said at the beginning of the intervention.

- **Express care and concern**. The leader must emphasize that all these people have gathered because they're concerned about the chemical dependent and want to talk to him about those concerns: "Bill, I know you're surprised to see us all here today, and I'll bet you're pretty frightened, too. We're here because we value you and want to talk to you. We want to let you know we all love you very much and are very concerned about what's happening to you. . . ."

- **Get the chemical dependent to agree not to respond until the people have all finished speaking.** This is crucial. If the chemically dependent person is allowed to respond or argue at will, the gradual, accumulating impact of the data, concern, and love will be dissipated. This request is best presented in a gentle manner rather than as a demand: "Now, I know you're going to want to respond to what you hear. However, I'm asking you to agree to let everyone say what they have to say first, and I promise you you'll have an opportunity to respond. Will you agree to that?"

- **Say exactly what the group wants the chemical dependent to do**. After all have finished their statements, the leader says exactly what they want the chemical dependent to do. Each person will already have expressed the desire that he get some help, but the specifics of that help are left until the end: "Bill, we all need help. We want you to join us. We have an interview set up with a counselor at Parkridge Treatment Center. Your bags are packed, and they have a bed ready for you. The staff is looking forward to working with you."

2) Decide the order in which the people will speak. This is crucial for the group to consider carefully. In general, family members, especially children, should speak after friends, employers, and others outside the immediate family have spoken. The first people help break down the barriers to listening to the data, although the family members' data is usually the most powerful. Their statements are often what convince the chemical dependent to accept treatment.

3) Decide on seating arrangements. Even the seating can be an important factor in intervention. Some guidelines are:
- Avoid having the chemical dependent sit near the door. This makes it too easy for the person to leave the room impulsively. If he or she is across the room and others are directly in front of the door, this presents a psychological though not a physical barrier to exiting.
- Have the leader or a close friend sit next to the chemical dependent.
- Avoid seating the spouse close to the chemical dependent. Otherwise it's easy for the person to direct his attention away from the group and to focus his anger and fear on the spouse.

4) Role-play the presentation of the data. First choose a concerned person to play the role of the chemical dependent; then have each of the others present his or her data.

Review the data carefully together, making sure that each group member:

- Expresses care and concern.
- Has prepared data in the manner described above.
- Avoids asking questions such as "Do you know how that makes me feel?" Such questions invite reactions from the chemical dependent and may lead to arguing.
- Concludes with a **general** statement about what he or she wants: "I want us to get help." "I want my dad back."

During the role-play, some group members will most likely start to express their anger, resentment, opinions, and judgments. Point out to them how destructive this can be to the intervention process. You can also help them work through their anger and other feelings at this time. Many concerned persons feel overwhelmed by their anger when they begin working on the intervention process. However, by talking it out with the others, including the counselor, or even role-playing it with the chemical dependent, they're able to deal sufficiently with it to allow them to go on and participate effectively in the process.

5) Clarify what they'll do if the person rejects every alternative. This is where **"power factors"** come into play. Remind your clients of their power and influence, and help them clarify what power they're willing to use. If a spouse feels the situation is so serious that she can't live with the alcoholic if he continues drinking, she has to be willing to make that commitment and stand by it. If an employer feels he has to fire a person unless that person goes to treatment (presuming that past promises to quit drinking or using have failed), the employer must be clear and firmly committed to that course of action. This is no place for bluffing or hedging. When a structured intervention has been so carefully planned out by a group of concerned persons, they must mean what they say. Even if the chemical dependent doesn't accept treatment this time, he may well accept it the next time. But the next intervention probably **won't** work if the credibility of the interveners has been called into question the first time. All concerned persons must decide exactly what they'll do if the person rejects every alternative, and must be willing to follow through with their decision. It's important to remember, however, that intervention isn't a power struggle between the family and other concerned persons and the chemically-dependent person. It's meant to be a respectful and caring description of the reality they must all face together and of the options available to them.

6) Decide where the intervention will take place. The actual intervention session should be held on neutral ground such as a professional's office. This can be the counselor's office, the chemical dependent's place of employment, his doctor's office, or a lawyer's office. It's strongly recommended that intervention **not** take place in the chemically dependent person's home; the home setting allows the person too many avenues to abort the process. He can simply walk into another room, turn on the television and stop listening, or order the group to leave his home. At an office, the reassurance and safety of home surroundings are taken away. The message is "Today is different. Today isn't like the other times you've heard this data in your own house. Today, we all have a matter of serious concern to deal with."

Before the actual intervention session, the professional should make certain that no phone calls or any other kinds of interruptions will disrupt the group. It's also important to instruct family members and other concerned persons to avoid laughing, joking, smoking cigarettes, drinking coffee or other beverages, or otherwise attempting to distract one another or the chemical dependent from the seriousness of the moment. The intervention session must be treated with seriousness and dignity.

The group also has to decide who will bring the person to the intervention site. Most often, the chemically dependent person is told clearly by a spouse or other relative that they have an appointment together to talk to a counselor about their family problems. This is a legitimate statement. Employers have held interventions, telling the employee that there are concerns about problems on the current project that need to be cleared up and that one of the concerns is how his drinking is interfering with the project.

The chemical dependent isn't always informed about every person who will be there. That can be overwhelming and may frighten him away. It's left to the counselor or group leader to address this issue when the session starts. For example, "Tom, I know you must be surprised to see us all here. We decided to meet together because every person in this room cares about you and is worried about you." Again, the person is surprised, perhaps even angry, when he sees a group waiting to meet with him. However, the expression of care, concern, and love is also very disarming and usually gets the group through that initial phase of the intervention session.

The Professional's Role in Facilitating the Intervention

Basically, your role as a professional during the intervention session is to make sure that the concerned persons do what they've prepared themselves to do. The extreme anxiety caused by the process will call for you to give a lot of reassurance and support, not only to the concerned persons, but to the chemical dependent as well.

You also serve as **advocate** for all present: the family members, concerned persons, and the chemical dependent.

On the day of the intervention, all concerned persons except the one bringing the chemical dependent to the meeting should arrive at least an hour ahead of time. This gives you a chance to make sure that the arrangements with the treatment center, the employer, and any other contingencies have been taken care of, and that everyone knows the agenda and his or her own part in the process.

Both chemical dependents and concerned persons react in many different ways to an actual intervention session. You may have to work with any or all of them during or after the intervention session to help them deal with their feelings.

During the intervention session emotions run high, and fear or anxiety can interfere with your best-laid plans. Your role as the professional is to help the group **stay on track** and stick to their plan. Here are some things to watch for:

- **Make sure the chemical dependent agrees not to respond until all the concerned persons have finished with their statements.** Don't let this slip by. Sometimes the group leader will be so nervous that he or she will move right into data-sharing without getting the person to agree to withhold his responses until the end. Also, more likely than not you'll have to remind the chemical dependent during the intervention session that he agreed not to respond until everyone had finished.

- **Watch for signs of fear in the chemical dependent.** Identify with the person as he or she gets threatened: e.g., "John, you look really frightened. I would be too if I were in your place. But remember, we're here because we **care** about you." Fear in the concerned persons should be recognized and addressed in a similar fashion.

- **Watch for enabling behavior on the part of the concerned persons.** Although all concerned persons have practiced making their statements, they've not done so in the presence of the chemical dependent. As he shows signs of hurt, fear, or anger, some members of the group may start to alter their approach by minimizing the impact that the drinking/drug use has had or by modifying the rehearsed presentation of data. Another concerned person may try to protect the chemical dependent. When this happens, you can make the person aware of that behavior by identifying with it: "Judy, I know you love Tom and don't want to see him hurt. But we're not here today to figure out **why** he drinks. We just want to let him know what his drinking is doing to him and to the people he loves." At that point you might move on to another concerned person or remind the person who's trying to protect the alcoholic of statements he or she made earlier in the session. Minimizing, modifying, or protective behavior by concerned persons almost always directly contradicts their previous statements of facts or feelings about the chemical use. This is another reason why having written lists is crucial.

- **Watch for surrender words.** It's very important that the professional listen for "surrender words," the subtle ways in which a chemical dependent indicates he's willing to accept treatment. Unless the counselor picks up on these surrender words, the intervention session can drag on longer than is necessary or effective. Chemical dependents don't usually say, "You're right. I see my drinking/using is creating problems for me and all of you, and I want to go to treatment." Rather, they usually give small, subtle, indirect hints that they've stopped denying the problem and have heard the group:

  "Boy, I don't know how I'm gonna tell my boss."
  "How do you think the kids will do without me?"
  "I'll never be able to take the time off from work."

When the chemical dependent gives one of these small hints, the leader doesn't have to respond to the concern raised, but rather should take such statements as signs that the person is open to accepting treatment. Even if not every last difficulty that might be raised by the chemical dependent has been worked out, the concerned persons can assure him they'll do all they can to take care of his worries. Also, the facilitator or one of the concerned persons can simply reemphasize that treatment for chemical dependence is the most important thing in his life right now.

When and if the person surrenders—i.e., has heard and accepted that he needs treatment—the intervention can end before everyone has presented their data. After all, the goal is to get the person to accept help. During the evaluation phase or family counseling phase of treatment, remaining data and feeling responses can and should be presented and worked through.

The treatment center of choice should be made aware immediately that the structured intervention has been held and told what has taken place. The treatment staff can use the momentum established during the intervention session to make assessment and treatment of the client progress effectively.

One thing the treatment staff must do is to process with the chemical dependent (and the spouse when possible) what happened during the intervention session and how they're feeling about it. If this is done during or shortly after admission, while the data is still fresh, a counselor can reinforce the chemical dependent's feelings of surrender or can help him express his anger or sense of betrayal, and can keep him mindful of how his chemical use is affecting his life. This is information that could otherwise take several weeks to bring out in the treatment process.

If the treatment center has a "concerned persons group" or a "family program," those who participated in the intervention could also participate in the treatment process. If not, the counselor can get a signed release from the chemical dependent—who's now a client of the treatment center—allowing the counselor to get critical information from the concerned persons who participated in the intervention.

The Professional's Role in Helping Concerned Persons Deal with the Results of the Intervention Session

A post-intervention session with concerned persons is recommended because no matter what happens in the intervention session, they'll need to be reminded that **intervention is a process, not an event.** If the chemical dependent agrees to go to treatment, the concerned persons still have to continue to share data, stop enabling, and work on not getting enmeshed again in counterproductive or dysfunctional behavior. They'll certainly need to do these things if the chemical dependent chooses to resume his alcohol/drug use.

Sometimes when the chemical dependent leaves immediately for treatment, several family members will accompany him. Those remaining with the counselor need the opportunity to share their feelings, summarize what they've learned, and consider what their role will be as the treatment progresses. It's also advisable to contact later the family members who accompanied the chemical dependent to treatment and help them process their feelings. They may even want to come back to the office to review that process and to get some closure to the intervention session.

If the person refuses to accept treatment or any of the stipulations of the concerned persons, remind the group of all they've learned about chemical dependence. The family, especially, needs your professional support and assurance that they're not responsible for the illness and that they must make decisions that aren't contingent on the chemically dependent person's behavior or approval. They have to go on with their own lives and follow through on the action plan they made prior to the intervention. This, of course, may require ongoing support from you. Remember that the concerned persons who contacted you are still your primary clients. The chemical dependent is now the client of the treatment center, but you have the right to stay closely involved; most reputable treatment centers will not only honor this right but will value the opportunity to keep you involved.

PART 3

A MODEL FOR
INTERVENTION
PROGRAMMING

Introduction

The kind of intervention described in this book can be practiced as a counseling technique by any helping-professional who has taken the trouble to learn about chemical dependence, its effects on the family, and the intervention process. However, if your agency, organization, or private practice deals with a large number of clients who have alcohol/drug-related problems, you may want to consider a **formal intervention program**. Such a program would provide the same information that you'd give to individual clients or families, but more of it would be imparted in larger, more formal group settings.

The purpose of placing clients together in classes and groups is not to "mass produce" the intervention process. Rather, there are very distinct advantages to having several families working together to learn about chemical dependence and what they can do about it. Let's consider how the group setting helps one aspect of intervention programming.

Some advantages of a group setting. The "Feeling Chart," outlined by Dr. Vernon E. Johnson in his book, *Intervention: How to Help Someone Who Doesn't Want Help*, describes the "emotional syndrome" of chemical dependence. It shows how feelings play an important role in the progression of alcoholism, and it details signs and symptoms that indicate a person is progressing from normal drinking to harmful dependence.

When intervention was first practiced at the Johnson Institute, the counselors had chalkboards in their offices and used the Feeling Chart as a diagnostic tool for family members. When the Feeling Chart is shown this way to a spouse or to one family, they inevitably will make comments about how their experience has followed a similar pattern. When this Feeling Chart exercise is formalized into a "group information session" for clients, it's even more powerful. Here are some reasons why:

- The group setting breaks down feelings of uniqueness and isolation and lowers the fear level of clients. They realize there are other people just like themselves with similar experiences, similar fears, similar hopes.
- The group session helps to dissipate the stereotyped image of chemically dependent persons and helps concerned persons see that there are many other "normal" people, people whom they look up to, who are facing the problem of alcohol/drug dependence.
- The group tends to motivate itself. Members encourage one another to participate in the process.
- Gathering together in groups to learn about chemical dependence and intervention provides a shared language that clients and professionals can use to talk about their problems. When a client talks about the delusions her spouse has, others will know what "delusion" means. When a person says that alcoholism is a "disease," they'll better understand what that person is talking about.

A variety of group formats can be used in a formal intervention program. Following are the basic components of the Intervention Program Model developed by the Johnson Institute.

Client Flow in an Intervention Program

A client in a typical formal intervention program would generally follow this pattern of service:

1. **Initial contact.** The client almost always calls the agency rather than walking in. The people who answer the phone must be well trained to deal with concerned persons. Concerned persons are generally suffering from emotional pain, are frightened and burdened with misinformation. Well-trained, caring people must be available to answer their initial questions, support them in their search for help, and

refer them to the next appropriate resource, usually the intake counselor.

2. **Intake counselor.** The intake counselor listens to the client's complaint, explains the services in a general fashion, and if there appears to be a suitable agency/client match, makes an appointment for the client to attend an information session.

3. **Information session.** This is a regularly scheduled group meeting for prospective clients to learn more about chemical dependence and what can be done about it before committing themselves to counseling sessions or to a formal program.

4. **Private session with an intervention counselor.** Generally a client meets with an assessment/intervention counselor after attending an information session where a decision is made as to whether the client should proceed to a **concerned persons group** or to **family intervention classes.**

5. **Concerned persons groups** are for those clients, usually spouses or children of alcohol/drug dependent persons, who are immobilized by their fear, shame, denial, and delusion. Often these concerned persons are so enmeshed in the disease process of chemical dependence that they've lost all perspective and find it difficult to accept or practice the basic tenets of intervention. They need special preliminary help to get stabilized.

6. **Family intervention classes.** These classes are for concerned persons who appear able and ready to begin work on planning an intervention.

7. **Pre-intervention session.** This is the final preparation/ practice session before the actual structured intervention session.

8. **Intervention session.** Family members and concerned persons participate in an actual structured intervention session with the chemical dependent.
9. **Post-intervention session.** This is a private session with the family and other concerned persons after the structured intervention session has concluded.

Following is a general overview of the structure and content of information sessions, the private session with an assessment/intervention counselor, concerned persons groups, family intervention classes and pre- and post-intervention sessions.

The Information Session

These sessions usually last about an hour and can be held two or three times per week at an agency or private counseling office. The content is simple and straightforward:

- The basics of the disease concept of chemical dependence.
- The Feeling Chart of Dr. Vernon Johnson: how the chemically dependent person's denial and delusion prevent him from seeing what his alcohol/drug use is doing to him and to others.
- How those living or working with a chemically dependent person are affected by the disease.
- Enabling: what it is and how concerned persons get caught up in these behaviors.
- A strong emphasis on treatment as effective, desirable, and available.
- Some general statements about intervention.

It's best not to say very much about intervention at the first information session; it tends to scare clients away. The details can be covered in later sessions.

Those attending the session should be given some supportive strokes simply for having the courage to seek help. The presenter should acknowledge that it's normal for participants to feel afraid, uncertain, and even guilty about the problems they're facing. Let them know that, no matter how they're feeling, they can credit themselves for having the courage to come to listen and learn, because millions of people around the world facing the same problems will never take action and will suffer unnecessarily.

Private Session with an Assessment/Intervention Counselor

At the end of the information session, ask the clients if they already have an appointment with an assessment/intervention counselor. This appointment can be made at the same time the appointment for the information session is made. If possible, it's best if everyone at the information session can talk with a counselor immediately afterward. During this private session the counselor should accomplish the following things:

- Review the ideas presented in the information session; be alert to how well the client was able to hear and accept the ideas.
- Help clients look at specific concerns about their current life situations.
- Assist in identifying the client's role in the specific concern.
- Determine if the family and the problem drinker/user are exhibiting symptoms associated with the disease of chemical dependence.
- Try to determine if an intervention is appropriate. Is the client ready and able, and does he or she have enough concerned persons ready to support an intervention process? Find out if other meaningful concerned persons

could be encouraged to come and talk with you or, prefera-
bly, come directly to the family intervention classes.

- Support the client in developing a plan of action.
- If the client didn't seem able to hear or accept the information about the disease process, is unwilling to contact concerned persons, or for any other reason appears emotionally immobilized or unstable, suggest a referral to the
  concerned persons group or other more appropriate care
  such as to a psychiatrist or psychologist.

The Concerned Persons Group

This group is designed to help those who for the present are
emotionally unstable or immobilized and not able or ready to
proceed with the intervention process. The concerned persons
group is also appropriate for those clients who feel isolated and
alone and still lack the support of family members or concerned
friends. A description of persons who are appropriate for this
group or class is contained in Parts I and II of the book *Diagnosing and Treating Co-dependence* by Timmen L. Cermak, M.D.,
published by the Johnson Institute. Those sections of the book
describe in detail specific criteria for defining and diagnosing co-
dependence. Some of those criteria as defined by Dr. Cermak
are:

**Continued investment of self-esteem in the ability to control
oneself and others in the face of serious adverse consequences.** Co-dependents tend to believe they can overcome
their own problems and the problems of a chemically dependent person by sheer force of will: e.g., "If only we all
try hard enough and pull together, we can get your father to
stop drinking." Since shame keeps them from reaching out
to others or admitting they have a problem and asking for

help, they try to solve the problem on their own, with the result that they become more and more isolated and dysfunctional.

Confusion of identities. Says Dr. Cermak: "The co-dependent's self-worth rises with his or her partner's success or failure." In the case of a co-dependent enmeshed in a painful relationship with a chemical dependent, that chemical dependent's inability to stop using alcohol/drugs is interpreted by the co-dependent as caused by the co-dependent's own personal inadequacy. "If I just try harder to get him to stop—he will."

Low self-esteem. Both a cause and effect of co-dependence, low self-esteem tends to lead these people into self-destructive relationships and to keep them stuck in those relationships, no matter how painful.

Assumption of responsibility for meeting others' needs to the exclusion of acknowledging one's own. A co-dependent can be literally worried sick that her husband isn't getting enough to eat, all the while maintaining a personal diet of cigarettes and coffee because she's too nervous to eat. She'll allow her husband and children to scream at her, but not at one another.

Anxiety and boundary distortions around intimacy and separation. "Picking up on others' feelings," says Dr. Cermak, "is rationalized as being 'sensitive.' The co-dependent involved with a chemical dependent actually feels that person's pain, rather than feeling empathy for the pain. This helps to fill the void which results from not honoring one's own needs and feelings."

Excessive reliance on denial. According to Dr. Cermak, "Co-dependents frequently see the breakdown of their denial system as a sign of their own personal inadequacy, much as chemical dependents view their growing lack of control over alcohol/drugs as a sign of personal weakness." The amount of delusion and denial maintained by a co-dependent can equal or exceed that of the chemically dependent person.

Constriction of emotions. "Typically," Dr. Cermak points out, "the emotions co-dependents work hardest to restrict are those normally considered to be immature, dangerous, uncomfortable, or just plain bad: anger, fear, sadness, rage, embarrassment, bitterness, loneliness, etc. Unfortunately, it is impossible to put a lid on such 'negative' feelings without also impeding the expression of more positive ones, such as happiness." This is one reason that the last part of the First Step of Al-Anon is so important to co-dependents: "We admitted that our lives had become unmanageable." Co-dependents are deeply dedicated to "managing their lives and the lives of others."

Depression. "Anger turned inward, unresolved grief, the chronic restraint of feelings, being identified more with one's false self than one's true self—co-dependents have plenty of reasons to be depressed," according to Dr. Cermak. "Typically, however, they view their depression as evidence of inadequacy and the failure to stay in control, and for this reason they usually deny its presence."

Hypervigilance. "The only way for the co-dependent to survive," according to Dr. Cermak, "is by being ultrasensitive to subtle shifts in a chemical dependent's behavior and mood. Such hypervigilance is a recognized symptom of post-traumatic stress disorder (PTSD), which is most typically seen in combat veterans."

Compulsions. Co-dependents tend to involve themselves in a great deal of anxiety-driven, compulsive behavior. They might overeat, overwork, gamble, or be compulsively involved in religion or religious ritual. Some watch television constantly and worry if they miss a segment of their favorite soap opera; others clean the house incessantly and obsessively in an attempt to forestall unwanted and uncomfortable feelings.

Substance abuse. Many co-dependents develop their own personal problems with alcohol, diet pills, tranquilizers, and other mood-altering substances with addictive potential.

Has been or is the victim of recurrent physical or sexual abuse. "Co-dependents tend to minimize both the amount of violence in their relationships and the level of stress that they live under," Dr. Cermak points out. "They do not see themselves as victims of physical or sexual abuse except in the most extreme cases, and even then they frequently take the blame: either they 'caused' the abuse, or they 'deserve' to be treated abusively."

Stress-related illness. Headaches (tension and migraine), asthma, hypertension, strokes, gastritis, peptic ulcers, spastic colon, rheumatoid arthritis, and sexual dysfunction are all more symptomatic with co-dependents than with the general population.

Content of the concerned persons group. The concerned persons group can help co-dependents and others by:
- Providing information about chemical dependence and co-dependence.
- Creating a supportive atmosphere in which clients are able to gain strength and understanding from others with similar problems.
- Creating an opportunity for clients to gain personal insights that can enable them to feel more comfortable with and respectful of themselves.
- Teaching the principles of intervention and encouraging participants (when able and ready) to proceed with an intervention with the chemically dependent person.

In Part III of *Diagnosing and Treating Co-dependence,* Dr. Cermak offers many more suggestions for working with co-dependents. The concerned persons group could be structured into a limited number of sessions or left open-ended. Some clients may need many months of group and individual work before they're ready to take even minor steps toward stopping their enabling behavior and starting intervention.

The concerned persons group should not become an end in itself. At times, we helping-professionals might actually find ourselves enabling co-dependents to stay in unhealthy relationships by prolonging counseling rather than getting down to the business of intervention and change.

The Family Intervention Classes

Family intervention classes are designed for family members, friends, or others concerned about someone's chemical use who are emotionally able and ready to participate in the intervention process. The classes provide:

- Information on the disease of chemical dependence.
- Information on the principles and dynamics of intervention.
- Support through relating to others with similar problems and circumstances.
- Tools needed to build a supportive, helping intervention team.
- Skill-building activities designed to assist families and other concerned persons to prepare for an actual structured intervention.

The material for family intervention classes can be delivered in a series of three evenings in a single week.

Session 1. The purpose of this session is to educate the family and concerned persons about the effects of chemical dependence on the chemical dependent and on themselves. It's also to help them recognize their "enabling behavior" so they'll be able to take some positive action. While much of the material from the original information session is repeated here, it will be new to many participants since they won't have been to that session. At this stage of the program, everything is action-oriented. Participants will be planning their own intervention process. Content includes:

- The Feeling Chart, delusion and denial, the issue of value conflicts, enabling, and family dysfunction.
- The signs and symptoms of chemical dependence: preoccupation, loss of control, tolerance, unpredictable mood-swings, blackouts, etc.
- Group discussions during which participants learn to share how they feel in order to help break through feelings of being different from other families and the isolation those feelings create. The large group can be broken down into smaller groups and asked questions such as: "How have delusion and denial affected you and your family?" "Have you seen delusion and denial in the chemically dependent person you're living with?" "Can you tell the group at least one way you've enabled a chemical dependent to keep drinking/using?"
- Information on the kinds of treatment available in the area. It isn't necessary for concerned persons to learn every detail about treatment. The important issue is that treatment is available and that it works. If you're presenting the information, offer examples of people who've made major changes in treatment and what this has meant for their families.
- The principles of intervention. This will be a much more detailed presentation than they've heard before. People in these sessions actually begin to write their lists of data and start planning just how they'll go about intervening.

Session 2. This session is almost entirely audiovisual. The participants view either the film "I'll Quit Tomorrow" or both "The Enablers" and "The Intervention." These films portray how chemical dependence progresses and how one can address it by effectively planning to use certain techniques. The facilitator can ask people to watch for enabling behaviors in the films and to observe how the techniques of intervention are employed.

Session 3. During this session, participants break up into several groups to role-play a successful, structured intervention, using simulated data. It isn't necessary for members of one family to stay in the same group for the role-play.

After the role-play, the facilitator gives participants feedback on how they've presented their data. The facilitator does this just as he or she would during the actual pre-intervention session role-play. The facilitator needs to make certain that the leader asks for an agreement from the chemical dependent to refrain from responding while the data is being presented. The facilitator also observes the concerned persons for use of such things as imprecise or vague data, inappropriate anger, minimizing, enabling, protecting, and modifying. Since the facilitator of this session isn't likely to catch every interaction in every group, it's recommended that participants also give one another feedback during this session.

The Pre-intervention Session

The purpose of this private session is to help clients make final preparations for the structured intervention. The basic format was described previously under "Guiding concerned persons through an intervention role-play" (p. 61).

The counselor should expect regression in some of the concerned persons at the pre-intervention session. This regression may be due to the paralyzing fear some are feeling, to doubts setting in about the feasibility of doing an intervention, or to the reemergence of old ways of thinking: "It's a moral problem"; "It's really my fault"; "He just has too many pressures in his life." The counselor is advised to do some reeducating at this time. Remind your clients of some of the information they've already listened to and agreed with. You may want to review with them the data they've gathered and the feelings they've already expressed about that data. In general, you can let them know that it's normal for them to feel some doubts and fears at this time and that it would be a rare group that didn't experience those feelings. However, be sure also to reinforce the feelings of hope they've expressed about the possibility of change in their lives, and encourage them to continue. Let them know they aren't expected to conduct themselves perfectly during the intervention, that you and the other concerned persons in the group will be there to support anyone who feels shaky or hesitant.

The Post-intervention Session

This is also a private session that takes place with the family and other concerned persons after the intervention. Whether or not the chemical dependent accepts treatment, this session is extremely important. The objectives of this session are:

1. To help the family process their feelings and reactions to the intervention.
2. To help them assess the data presented, what was omitted, what still needs to be shared and when, what problems they may encounter in the future, and how they'll be handled.
3. To help them make choices for their continued recovery as individual family members regardless of the response or reaction of the chemical dependent.
4. To give them an opportunity to decide upon and begin to practice new behaviors, now and in the future, and to validate their courage and commitment.

5. To help them reflect on and review what happened in the intervention as a result of their group effort.

The post-intervention session also gives the counselor and the family an opportunity to celebrate what they've accomplished on several levels: 1) helping the chemical dependent accept treatment; 2) helping themselves to be more aware of their power to make effective choices for themselves, whether the chemical dependent accepts treatment or not; 3) learning to practice new and constructive behaviors to ensure their own progress in recovery.

The family and concerned others should be reminded that **intervention is a process, not a single event,** and that now is the time to outline what significant changes have been made and what other changes need to be made as the process continues. It's recommended that these changes be outlined on a chalkboard or flip chart so the family can actually see where they were before, where they are now, and where they're headed as a result of taking action through intervention. Some examples of changes that families usually point out are:

1. Before, they felt they had few rights as individuals and as family members; now they know they have rights and can exercise them without feeling guilty or disloyal.
2. Before, their boundaries as persons were blurred or maybe nonexistent; now they've learned how to set boundaries and limits for themselves within the family and with others.
3. Before, they assessed and judged themselves by external factors (how others would react); now they have their own internal system for validation.
4. Before, they may have felt that only certain members of the family were valued and important in the family system; now each family member feels equally valued and important.

5. Before, they acted dishonestly as individuals and as a family; now they can speak out honestly and value themselves for it.
6. Most importantly: before, the family felt hopeless; now they feel hopeful.

The family needs to realize that together they've recognized and confronted a painful issue and dealt honestly with it. This "before" and "after" awareness helps them realize that they've acted effectively as a group to solve a painful problem and can do it again and again because they've finally learned to tap their own resources and strengths.

The post-intervention session also allows the counselor to bring a sense of closure to the intervention. This doesn't mean that those persons who had some of their own personal issues raised during the process have had them resolved. Instead they'll need to be encouraged to continue in a personal recovery program to address their own and other family issues as well as to learn to live comfortably in a healthy family system.

The post-intervention session also teaches the family how to deal with separation: the temporary separation from their chemically dependent person, and the separation from the counselor upon whom they've usually come to depend. The family members need to be encouraged and assisted to make a smooth transition into the appropriate counseling, therapy, or self-help resource, whether this means a family treatment program, psychotherapy, individual counseling, Al-Anon, Adult Children of Alcoholics' Groups, or similar programs. Families will at times want to give credit to the counselor for the process. **This is an opportunity for the counselor to give that credit back to the family, to validate the choice they've made to use their rightful power to begin to restore themselves to health**.

The post-intervention session is very important to the intervention process, regardless of the outcome for the chemical dependent. It should be scheduled **before** the actual structured intervention takes place, usually during the last family meeting.

The intervention program model described here has been used by the Johnson Institute for over twenty years. It has been used effectively by thousands of widely diverse counseling agencies, clinics, treatment centers, and other organizations, and by helping-professionals in private practice. The model as described in this book is of course ideal; but it **can** be and most often **is** modified and adapted by helping-professionals to suit their particular cultural, social, logistical, and economic settings and circumstances.*

---

* The Johnson Institute, through its yearly seminar series and custom-designed training seminars, provides a number of different Intervention Training Seminars for helping-professionals. Many of these Intervention Seminars provide practical assistance for adapting and modifying this formal intervention program model to suit their particular needs. For more information, write the Director of Training, Johnson Institute, 510 First Avenue North, Minneapolis, MN 55403, or call 1-800-231-5165. In Minnesota, call 1-800-247-0484.

PART 4

SPECIAL ISSUES
AND CONCERNS
WITH INTERVENTION

Since the practice of intervention was developed more than twenty years ago, it has been used by helping-professionals in many different situations and with many different types of clients. The experience of these professionals has raised a number of issues and concerns about the use of the intervention process. In this section we will address some of the most commonly recurring questions.

How does intervention work with different populations?

The technique of intervention was initially developed for use with a particular profile of persons: married, middle-class, middle-aged males. This doesn't mean, however, that it hasn't worked well with other groups. Many women and minority group members have benefited from the same techniques described in this book.

As the entire chemical dependence field begins to address previously under-served populations, all professionals will have to review their approaches and modify them when necessary. For instance, chemical dependents who are physically disabled, victims of abuse, single mothers, or members of other minority groups all have different needs. It's been very helpful to the field of chemical dependence to have recovered alcoholics/addicts working in the field and developing techniques to serve people like themselves. Similarly, professionals who are physically disabled, victims of abuse, single mother alcoholics/addicts, and members of minority groups will be best able to take the basic material presented here, apply it in special situations, and learn what works best in those special situations.

As was mentioned earlier, however, there are situations in which intervention might not be appropriate. If an alcoholic also batters his wife, she may be taking too great a risk to attempt an intervention. A counselor shouldn't counsel the woman to attempt an intervention in the expectation that, if the alcoholic goes to treatment, she won't have to worry about being abused anymore. Not all battering can be directly related to chemical dependence.

When spouses are involved in bitter divorce settlements or custody battles, one spouse shouldn't be initiating an intervention on the other. The trust level between them would be too low for carrying out a caring, concerned, nonjudgmental approach.

When a chemical dependent or any of the concerned persons is suicidal, intervention should be postponed until the safety of each person can be reasonably assured.

Can we use the same process with adolescents?

This intervention model has been used with adolescents, but experience has proven that intervention with teenagers is a more difficult and complex process than with adults. For example, interventions that have been done with adolescents who abuse alcohol/drugs haven't always clearly resulted in a diagnosis of chemical dependence. Nor have they always required or resulted in an adolescent's going to treatment. With adolescents, we need to begin the intervention process earlier because **chemical use by itself** has great legal implications for adolescents. Moreover, if an adolescent doesn't have a long history of chemical use or if he hasn't demonstrated an inability to stop using, a structured intervention would be premature. If a young person is caught using drugs on or near the school grounds, for instance, it's better to use the school disciplinary process coupled with some education about the effects of chemical abuse rather than a major intervention process followed by treatment. For a comprehensive treatment of how parents and professionals can use intervention successfully with adolescents, read *Choices and Consequences: How to Use Intervention with Teenagers in Trouble with Alcohol/Drugs, A Step-By-Step Guide for Parents and Professionals* by Dick Schaefer, published by the Johnson Institute.*

Is surprise really a big factor?

Some people have criticized the intervention approach as "sneaky" or "demeaning" because it appears to go behind the back of the chemical dependent. As was mentioned earlier, intervention does **not** have to be a complete surprise to the chemically dependent person. In many cases the chemically dependent person knows for weeks that his spouse is going for counseling and that the counseling has to do with concerns about alcohol/drug use problems in the home. In the treatment of mental illness, "transparency"—the fact that patients are often aware of the doctor's strategy for their recovery and the techniques the doctor will use to help them recover—isn't necessarily a hindrance to treatment. In dealing with chemical dependents, it's probably

---

* This book is designed to be a companion piece to the film entitled *Choices and Consequences: Intervention with Youth in Trouble with Alcohol/Drugs,* also produced by the Johnson Institute. The film dramatically portrays how parents and professionals working together can use the process of intervention to deal successfully with all levels of teenage chemical use. For more information, see Part 5, Further Resources for Programming.

not as necessary as many of us think to keep it a "secret" that an intervention is being planned. Often the chemical dependent is not only aware of the plan but attempts to curb his alcohol/drug use temporarily, most likely in anticipation of some form of confrontation.

In planning an intervention, it's very important that you, as a professional, do not allow yourself to be pressured into using techniques you're uncomfortable with or that are incompatible with your own professional philosophy or methods. If you believe that the chemical dependent should be made aware that his chemical use has become the focus of the counseling sessions for his family and others, you must act accordingly. If you believe he or she should also know who will be at the intervention session, then stand by your beliefs. Over time, you'll probably find that your approach works fine in certain situations. Those kinds of situations, then, are the ones in which you, as a professional, should agree to be involved as a facilitator.

What if I can't get concerned persons together for several weeks? What if I have only four hours to do this?

Sometimes it's very difficult to get the key concerned persons together for an intervention. In some instances, a key person has actually lived several thousand miles away and has been willing to participate in the intervention only if the time was convenient and limited. In these cases, professionals have had to break the intervention process down to its bare essentials. For example, the education portion of the process could be cut down to a one-hour talk on Dr. Vernon Johnson's "Feeling Chart" and the delusional system of the chemical dependent. Concerned persons would have to write their lists of data in a short time and practice the intervention quite briefly. Sometimes a concerned person who will be in town only for a short time can be sent some literature ahead of time and engaged in telephone conversations to help prepare him or her for the intervention process.

This can work if there are no serious impediments such as a severely co-dependent spouse, a friend who decides he's going to support the chemical dependent against the spouse, or great fear or hesitation on the part of many of the concerned persons to take action so quickly. Experience has shown that many hastily prepared interventions aren't successful and should be tried only if the seriousness of the chemically dependent person's condition warrants it and if all other options have been exhausted.

In any event, it's critical for the professional to use his or her experience and good judgment in deciding each case, keeping in mind that the primary purpose of intervention is to get the chemically dependent person the help he invariably needs, before it's too late.

My clients who are members of Al-Anon will say they have no need to intervene because they've "detached" from the problem.

The Al-Anon program is extremely effective. It helps those living with a chemically dependent person realize they're **not** the cause of the alcohol/drug use, that they're **not** responsible for the chemical dependent's behavior, and that they must carry on with their lives regardless of what the chemically dependent person does with his. Some spouses and other family members misinterpret the Al-Anon message as meaning that the chemically dependent person is sick from a disease and therefore not responsible for his behavior. They seek to be detached from the problems of the chemical dependent but instead become passive. They appear not to grasp that the second part of the Serenity Prayer, "the courage to change the things I can," implies that sometimes one must take direct action with the chemically dependent person.

To deal effectively with such clients, it's necessary to be very familiar with the Al-Anon literature. In it are many statements urging people to "change what can be changed" before they "accept the things that cannot be changed." Compassion dictates that you carefully confront spouses of chemical dependents on their misinterpretations or distortions of the Al-Anon message. You might share with them, for instance, that the fact that a person isn't responsible for having a disease doesn't mean he isn't responsible for failing to follow prescribed medical advice.

A client who's extremely co-dependent will probably continue to distort the Al-Anon message even after the basic concepts have been clarified again and again. This client needs to be confronted each time he or she engages in such thinking or behavior and be shown a healthier way of looking at the situation.

Who pays for intervention? Will insurance companies pay for it if they pay for treatment?

Unfortunately, interventions that take place prior to treatment are seldom paid for by insurance companies. Perhaps the day will come when intervention itself will be seen as an extremely important contribution to the health-care delivery system and be reimbursable in its own right.

If the spouse of a chemical dependent comes to a clinic for anxiety or marriage problems, treatment for those issues may be covered under her insurance policy. If such is the case, it's likely that the counseling required to prepare for a structured intervention would also be reimbursable should the anxiety, stress, or marriage problems be caused by a spouse's or other family member's chemical abuse.

Do we always have to work so hard to *create* a crisis for an alcoholic? What about piggybacking on an existing crisis?

If an alcoholic who has been denying his problem for years has just had a serious, alcohol-related accident, it might be best to move in immediately with an intervention rather than waiting several weeks to develop the process more methodically. Such self-made crises can be golden opportunities, times when the alcoholic is more open to hearing data he's refused to hear in the past. No matter what the situation, however, the more closely the interveners follow the process and methods described in this book, the better the chances of success. Even if a chemical dependent has just caused a serious accident, been fired, or upset some people terribly, **specific data, rehearsed and shared by meaningful concerned persons in an objective, caring, nonjudgmental way**, is still the most effective approach.

What about intervention after a person has entered treatment? What's the point of doing it then?

No matter at what stage a person is in the recovery process, he'll progress more rapidly if his view of his chemical dependence and its effects on others is based on **reality**. Reality, even to a sober alcoholic, isn't always self-evident. The program of Alcoholics Anonymous urges him to make a list of the persons he's harmed, but he may be genuinely unaware of whom he's harmed and in what ways. When family members and friends join him in treatment to detail the effects of his behavior, this is a form of intervention even though the focus is no longer on the immediate goal of entering treatment but on the long-term goal of recovery.

How can professionals protect themselves from legal liability when doing intervention work?

Keep in mind that your client is the concerned person who comes to you for help. This key client and the other concerned persons will do the actual intervention. The professional's role is to evaluate the data gathered by the client and other concerned persons to determine whether intervention is appropriate, and to prepare these persons to do the intervention. It's wise, however, for an organization or a professional in private practice to have a written policy that clearly states the role of the professional in intervention work. For example, that role may be stated in a way that emphasizes the professional's role in intervention as educator, evaluator, and facilitator. In addition, an organization or a professional in private practice can make it standard procedure to keep xeroxed copies of the concerned persons' written lists of data with their key client's file. Legal problems rarely arise around the intervention process, but these practical suggestions can help alleviate your concern about them. Remember, intervention is a process, not an event. And you as a professional are contracted to provide the service of educating, evaluating, and facilitating this process.

What if the intervention doesn't work? What do I tell the family and concerned persons?

If the chemical dependent doesn't agree to accept help and won't even agree to a "what if" clause, tell your clients not to give up; they need to keep on trying. Assure them that the chemical dependent's life will probably depend on their commitment to continue sharing their concerns and feelings about his alcohol/drug abuse. Over twenty years of experience at the Johnson Institute has shown that intervention tends to have a cumulative effect. If the first structured intervention session doesn't motivate the chemical dependent to accept treatment, the second probably will – or the third. Sometimes it takes even more effort on the part of the family and other concerned persons to break through the chemical dependent's defense system.

Alcoholics Anonymous wisely states that "there are men and women who are constitutionally incapable of being honest with themselves...they are not at fault; they seem to have been born that way. They are naturally incapable of grasping and developing a manner of living which demands rigorous honesty."

But what of the "incorrigible" alcoholic/addict, or the one who walks out of the structured intervention and never comes back, or the one who is "too far gone" for help? If that person continues drinking or using and never enters treatment, has intervention failed? The answer is no. In fact, according to Dr. Vernon Johnson, father of the intervention process, "**properly done**, intervention works every time; **properly done**, there are no failures." Here are some reasons why:

- The family members and other concerned persons who do the intervening are forever changed. They know they are not alone. They know that help and support are available to them. Their lives are never the same afterward.

- The family system is also changed, from one that was immobilized, fearful, guilty, shame-ridden and dysfunctional to one that has become open, honest, caring, self-respecting, and dedicated to recovery. Family members now know what chemical dependence is. They can recognize its symptoms **in themselves**, and they know how to get help **for** themselves.

- Finally, the chemical dependent himself is changed in relation to his alcohol/drug use. The crack in his wall of defenses has admitted knowledge that he will never again be able to fully deny. He will never be able to enjoy drinking or using again with impunity. (As one family member remarked, "At least we spoiled his drinking!")

In summary, intervention always has **some** effect, and that effect is almost invariably positive. At the very least, it offers a chance for recovery where before none existed; at most, it starts the whole family on the path toward fully living again.

PART 5

FURTHER RESOURCES FOR PROGRAMMING

Programming for intervention involves many issues about clients, chemical dependence, and the intervention process that can't be covered in a single book. The following Johnson Institute materials are useful additional resources for helping-professionals who want to develop formal intervention programs for their treatment center, agency, organization, or private practice.

Books

INTERVENTION: How to Help Someone Who Doesn't Want Help, A Step-By-Step Guide for Families and Friends of Chemically Dependent Persons by Vernon E. Johnson, D.D. This book is written especially for families and friends of chemical dependents but is also helpful to professionals. It provides a thirty-question quiz that concerned persons can use to determine if a loved one is chemically dependent. It teaches how the disease progresses; how to prepare for intervention and why; how to conquer reluctance; how to find out and assess treatment options; how to do an intervention; and how to get help for oneself. Dr. Johnson also shows how chemical dependence affects those around the sick person—spouses, children, neighbors, co-workers. He points out that intervention isn't a clinical process, but a **personal** one that brings families back together.

DIAGNOSING AND TREATING CO-DEPENDENCE: A Guide for Professionals Who Work with Chemical Dependents, Their Spouses and Children by Timmen L. Cermak, M.D. This book provides a framework for understanding co-dependence— a framework that interfaces directly with accepted psychiatric/ psychologic concepts, language, and diagnostic systems. Dr. Cermak presents clear diagnostic criteria and illustrates them with examples. He describes ways of treating co-dependence that go far beyond those currently in use and provides a section on Special Concerns with Children and Adult Children of Alcoholics.

CHOICES AND CONSEQUENCES: How to Use Intervention with Teenagers in Trouble with Alcohol/Drugs, A Step-By-Step Guide for Parents and Professionals by Dick Schaefer. This book teaches parents and professionals about chemical dependence, how teenage alcohol/drug dependence differs from that of adults, and why. It provides specific criteria for determining the level of a teenager's chemical involvement: experimental use; misuse; abuse and harmful dependence. In addition, it provides specific guidelines for effective communication, interaction, parenting and/or supervision of teenagers who have become harmfully involved with chemicals. It explains the delusional system of teenage chemical dependents and provides clear, specific instructions as well as effective techniques and strategies for using the process of intervention to deal successfully with this problem.

DIFFERENT LIKE ME: A Book for Teens Who Worry About Their Parents' Use of Alcohol/Drugs. This book, written expressly for teenagers as well as for concerned adults, describes how it feels to live with parents who abuse alcohol or other drugs. It's also a book about chemical dependence: what it is and what it does to people. In it, teenagers will find the answers they need to questions they may have asked, questions they may have wanted to ask, and questions they may have been afraid to ask. They'll also learn that they aren't alone, that they aren't responsible for their parents' alcohol/drug problem, that they can't make them well but that they should and **can** get help for themselves.

ALCOHOLISM IN THE PROFESSIONS by LeClair Bissell, M.D., and Paul W. Haberman. This book focuses on alcoholic men and women in professions. It offers the first published data on alcoholism among attorneys, physicians, nurses, dentists, and social workers. It shows how national organizations representing the groups studied and other major professions have addressed the problem of alcoholism and intervention for alcoholism within their ranks. It also contains an international directory of support, advocacy, and disciplinary groups for alcoholic professionals, along with information on membership requirements and contacts.

Booklets

The following booklets offer valuable information to professionals and concerned persons who need to learn more about chemical dependence; what it's like to live with a chemical dependent; intervention; and treatment.

Alcoholism: A Treatable Disease. A straightforward, readable look at the disease of chemical dependence, the confusion and delusion that accompany it, and the process of intervention. Its core message—alcoholism is treatable—offers hope to all concerned persons.

The Dynamics of Addiction by George A. Mann, M.D. This booklet explains some of the physical and psychological aspects of addiction and describes how addiction develops and continues. A special section on the children of alcoholics identifies family history and stress as important contributors to the cycle of chemical dependence.

How It Feels to Be Chemically Dependent by Evelyn Leite. Everyone who has anything to do with chemical dependence or co-dependence should read this booklet. It describes in a powerful way the psychological and emotional pain a chemically dependent person experiences as his disease progresses. Recovering persons and those who are just beginning to face their chemical dependence will see themselves and know they're not alone. Alcohol/drug dependent persons who haven't yet confronted their problem will recognize truths they can't deny. Family members and friends of alcohol/drug dependents will arrive at a clearer understanding of the emotional effects of chemical dependence. And helping-professionals will gain new insights into the feeling side of the disease.

Blackouts and Alcoholism by Lucy Barry Robe. What are blackouts, what causes them, and who has them? What do people do during blackouts? This booklet provides clear, understandable answers to these and other questions about blackouts and describes how blackouts can be used as critical data in interventions with chemically dependent persons.

Supervisors and Managers as Enablers by Brenda R. Blair, M.B.A. The author explores reasons why, even though supervisors might have training in identifying troubled employees, they actually still may be enabling the employee who has an alcohol/drug-related problem. She then gives supervisors specific ways to stop enabling and to start helping the employee.

The Family Enablers. Family members sincerely want to help the alcoholic. Instead, they often make things worse. By not dealing directly with their loved one's alcoholism, they enable him or her to progress to more serious stages of the disease. This booklet identifies and addresses this problem and points the way toward whole-family recovery.

Why Haven't I Been Able to Help? Spouses of alcohol/drug dependents become trapped in the disease of chemical dependence. Their self-image deteriorates. They fall victim to their own defenses. They exhibit a wide range of destructive behaviors ranging from controlling to enabling. This booklet looks closely at these behaviors—which can be changed—and at the promise of recovery through intervention.

Chemical Dependence: Yes, You Can Do Something. This booklet gives families of chemical dependents the basic knowledge they need to help their loved ones **now**. It covers the disease concept, denial, delusion, how the family is affected, enabling, intervention, and the hope of recovery. It's an ideal booklet for clients who attend information sessions about chemical dependence and intervention.

Detachment: The Art of Letting Go While Living with an Alcoholic by Evelyn Leite. Those living with an alcohol/drug dependent must learn to take responsibility for themselves, not for the drinker. This booklet tells how to rebuild the self in ways that can restore healthy thinking and lead to serenity, freedom, and peace.

Chemical Dependence and Recovery: A Family Affair. This booklet focuses on the family involved with chemical dependence. Topics include the disease and its phases within the family; the feelings of family members; enabling; co-dependence; intervention; treatment and recovery.

Recovery of Chemically Dependent Families. Many of the problems of recovering families are caused by their high expectations. They assume that once sobriety is attained, the family will go "back to normal" and stay there forever. Or they fear that the chemical dependent will return to using alcohol/drugs. This booklet examines these issues and explores how the family can learn to communicate and recover together.

Can I Handle Alcohol/Drugs? A Self-Assessment Guide for Youth by David Zarek and James Sipe. Written expressly for adolescents, this guide is sensitive to their feelings, needs, and level of maturity and helps them realistically assess how using chemicals can harm—or is already harming—them in the major areas of their lives. The guide reveals patterns of chemical use, misuse, abuse or dependence that help determine 1) the severity of the problem, 2) obstacles to recovery, and 3) options for referral or treatment. By appealing to teenagers' own personal experience, the guide evokes thinking and feeling responses that motivate them to change. A real eye-opening experience for teens.

Films

I'll Quit Tomorrow. Color, in three parts, 30 minutes each. This film provides a clear and thorough introduction to the disease concept of alcoholism, enabling, the intervention process, treatment, and the hope of healing and recovery. It's ideal both for information sessions in intervention programs and for treatment programs.

The Feeling Chart: The Dynamics of Alcoholism. Color, 33 minutes. This film featuring Dr. Vernon E. Johnson, founder and president emeritus of the Johnson Institute, is an indispensable tool for teaching families and friends why chemical dependents are unable to see what their alcohol/drug use is doing to themselves and to others. It's also very useful for teaching chemical dependents how their thoughts and feelings have been distorted by alcohol/drug abuse and why intervention and treatment are successful.

The Enablers. Color, 23 minutes. This film portrays the story of Jan, wife, mother, career woman—and alcoholic. Her family, friends, and employer are caught in the trap of protecting her from the consequences of her actions. Without knowing it, they're actually **enabling** her disease to progress, and they're suffering along with her. Arguments, embarrassments, fear, and anger have become part of their everyday lives. This film puts the problem of enabling into perspective and teaches concerned persons how to stop hurting and start helping.

The Intervention. Color, 28 minutes. A sequel to **The Enablers,** this is a classic film with a powerful message. It shows what happens when concerned persons around Jan, an alcoholic, decide to take positive action. Motivated by love and concern, they agree to work with a counselor and participate in an intervention. It isn't easy for any of them, but it works—and Jan takes the first step toward recovery. The film realistically depicts some of the difficulties and rewards of intervention. It illustrates what's involved in the process and demonstrates how **any** concerned person can help.

Choices and Consequences: Intervention with Youth in Trouble with Alcohol/Drugs. Color, 33 minutes. This film demonstrates how the process of intervention can be used to deal successfully with adolescents in trouble with alcohol/drugs. Parents and professionals not only learn how intervention works but will be motivated to initiate and participate in intervention and support networks in their communities. **Choices and Consequences** is ideal for teaching adolescents, too. The film shows them 1) that when they choose to use alcohol/drugs they must accept responsibility for the consequences; 2) that their personal choice to use alcohol/drugs can profoundly affect and even harm others; 3) how to use their knowledge of the different levels of alcohol/drug use to assess their own use and that of their friends; 4) that their own willingness to share concern about a friend in trouble with alcohol/drugs can really make a difference; and 5) how they can play an effective role in an intervention and support network.

For more information or to order any of these materials, call or write:

Johnson Institute
510 First Avenue North
Minneapolis, MN 55403-1607
1-800-231-5165
In Minnesota, 1-800-247-0484

AFTERWORD

Finally . . . A prayer of courage and wisdom:

"God, grant me the serenity to accept the things I cannot change,
The courage to change the things I can,
And the wisdom to know the difference."

For many years now, these three powerful lines have provided a foundation for daily living to millions of members of Alcoholics Anonymous, Al-Anon, and other self-help groups. The prayer is clearly a work of inspired genius. Everyone who reads it can say, "Yes, yes. If I could do that, my life would be happy, my days would flow smoothly, my heart would be at peace."

While it's known as the "Serenity Prayer," the title doesn't really do it justice. For this brief invocation has as much to do with courage and wisdom as it does with serenity.

Though God may grant to some a spontaneous and self-sustaining serenity, serenity comes to most of us only **after** we've done all we can; **after** we've faced our problems, examined our strengths and weaknesses, and made the changes in our lives that may calm the tempest and bring us peace.

For people living with a chemical dependent, serenity seldom comes before action—action to change whatever **can** and **needs to be** changed in their lives. This indeed takes wisdom and courage. And this is where helping-professionals, such as psychiatrists, psychologists, medical doctors, chemical dependence counselors, family and marriage therapists, social workers, nurses, members of the clergy, employee assistance counselors, lawyers, teachers, and others come into the picture.

We helping-professionals can't give our clients wisdom. But we can help them acquire insight, new perspective, and knowledge. We can help them examine their lives and the circumstances affecting their lives so they can benefit from experience. We can help them see the choices they face and encourage them to make healthy, constructive ones.

Neither can we give our clients courage. We can, however, help them examine their fears, dissect those fears to find their roots, determine how realistic the fears are and how to overcome them. We can work to free our clients from the paralyzing guilt and shame that keep them bound tightly in painful and harmful co-dependent relationships. We can help them accept the truth that courage doesn't come as a bolt out of the blue, but in painfully small increments. Our clients gradually come to accept that action is necessary, that change is possible. They try one small step, then another. When they find that their lives don't fall apart, they try bigger steps and do so more frequently.

Serenity comes to them when they know they've done all they can; when they know they've acted with courage and compassion; when they know they've reached out to others and gratefully accepted all the help and support their families and communities have to offer; when they know they've dug deep within themselves and found their own personal resources and strength.

The helping-professional is an intermediary in this process. We do what we can to help those living with chemically dependent persons to draw upon their own potential for wisdom, courage, and serenity. We facilitate a process that their own individual, social, and spiritual resources will bring to fruition. Our role in intervention, then, is like that described by an early pioneer in the field of medicine:

"I bind their wounds; God heals them."

When the Johnson Institute first opened its doors in 1966, few people knew or believed that alcoholism was a disease. Fewer still thought that anything could be done to help the alcohol/drug dependent person other than to wait for him or her to "hit bottom" and then pick up the pieces.

We've spent over twenty years spreading the good news that chemical dependence is a *treatable* disease. Through our publications, films, audiocassettes, seminars, and special services, including training and consultation, we've given hope and help to hundreds of thousands of people across the country and around the world. The intervention and treatment methods we've pioneered have saved lives, healed relationships, and brought families back together.

Today the Johnson Institute is a nationally recognized leader in the field of chemical dependence intervention, treatment, and recovery. Individuals, organizations, and businesses, large and small, rely on us to provide them with the tools they need. Schools, universities, hospitals, and treatment centers look to us for experience, expertise, innovation, and results. We plan to continue reaching out to chemically dependent people, their families, and the professionals who serve them.

To find out more about us, write or call:

510 First Avenue North
Minneapolis, MN 55403-1607
1-800-231-5165
In MN: 1-800-247-0484
or 341-0435

Need a copy for a friend?
You may order directly.

HOW TO USE INTERVENTION IN YOUR PROFESSIONAL PRACTICE

A Guide for Helping-Professionals Who Work
with Chemical Dependents and Their Families

Johnson Institute Books
Professional Series

$8.95

Order Form

Please send _____ copy (copies) of HOW TO USE INTERVENTION IN YOUR
PROFESSIONAL PRACTICE.

Price $8.95 per copy. Please add $1.00 shipping for the first book and 25¢ for
each additional copy.

_____
Name (please print)

_____
Address

_____
City/State/Zip

_____( )_____
Attention   *Telephone*

Please note that orders under $15.00 must be pre-paid.

If paying by credit card, please complete
the following:

☐ Bill the full payment to my credit card.
☐ VISA ☐ MasterCard ☐ American Express

Credit card number: _____

For MASTERCARD:
Write the 4 digits below the account number: _____

Expiration date: _____ Signature on card: _____

Return this order form to: The Johnson Institute
                            510 First Avenue North
                            Minneapolis, MN 55403-1607

For faster service, call our
Order Department TOLL-FREE:
1-800-231-5165

In Minnesota call:
1-800-247-0484

Ship to (if different from above):

Name _____

Address _____

City/State/Zip _____